"The world needs meditation on love: youth needs it, married couples need it, we all need it. Coming from Father Kennedy, such a meditation becomes well-nigh indispensable reading. His reputation as a psychologist of unusual spiritual insight has been well established through his books and other writings.

If one word could sum up the quality of love Father Kennedy most emphasizes, it would be *maturity*. This is not primarily a matter of chronological age but has everything to do with selflessness, patience, and altruism; in a word, it is the gospel of our Lord. Stressing the need for taking man as he is in his thousand little daily situations, the author exhibits a compassion, an understanding of real life, which is rare and of great value. He expands, in chapter after chapter, on Saint Paul to the Corinthians. Never has the relevance of that two-thousand-year-old letter been better demonstrated.

The book abounds in insights. Young people need to read it, including as it does a devastating indictment of our current romanticism with its psychedelic self-seeking and its inability to wait . . . The treatment of sex is likewise excellent: man in general, with his new-found freedom, is in a sort of adolescent stage and has yet to integrate his sexuality with friendship and love . . .

Older people, married and celibate, will appreciate the call to abandon narcissism and those bitter little triumphs and to get back to the business of really loving. A well-developed sense of one's own identity and worth is a prelude to this genuine love, and the author helps us see the danger of counterfeits like passivity and that brutal frankness which masquerades as truth. Few have written about friendship and love as well as this author has. His book is a universal gift."

—*The Sign*

A TIME FOR LOVE

Eugene C. Kennedy

IMAGE BOOKS

A DIVISION OF DOUBLEDAY & COMPANY, INC.

GARDEN CITY, NEW YORK

IMAGE BOOKS EDITION 1972
BY SPECIAL ARRANGEMENT
WITH DOUBLEDAY & COMPANY, INC.
IMAGE BOOKS EDITION PUBLISHED FEBRUARY, 1972

There is a season for everything, a time for every occupation under heaven . . . *a time for loving.*

Ecclesiastes 3:1, 8

Love is always patient and kind; it is never jealous; love is never boastful or conceited; it is never rude or selfish; it does not take offense, and it is not resentful. Love takes no pleasure in other people's sins but delights in the truth; it is always ready to excuse, to trust, to hope, and to endure whatever comes.

Love does not come to an end.

1 Corinthians 13:4–8

CONTENTS

A TIME FOR LOVE

INTRODUCTION

Walk across the Boston Common in the afternoon shadows when the office workers flood down from the State House. In every face you see a longing for love. Forget for a moment the supposed romance of San Francisco. Look rather at the impassive faces of the passengers clustered on the cable cars. Each one seems to be waiting to be lighted up by love. All the imagery of man in our age gives the same message. The most unlikely face, the fierce scowl of a red-neck sheriff, the glazed eyes of the man gone on drugs, the unravaged innocence of a child: In all these you sense man's deep loneliness and his hunger for closeness with others.

There is always something touching about man, even when he disguises his need for love behind the primitive mask of hatred and aggression. Even when man is at his worst, he is telling us how bewildered he is when he has lost touch with the values that make him truly human. I am writing this book in hopes that it will help men who have lost their way to find it again in friendship and love.

Only the most naïve author would think that he could solve the problems of the human race with his words. This is particularly true when you think for a moment about all the words that have been written or spoken about love. There is nothing we humans talk about more, no subject about which we give out so many subtle signs of yearning, and, at the same time, no subject with which we have more difficulty in the practical order of things. I suppose it is because it is so much easier than doing something about love in our lives that we talk and write so much of it.

Why is it that a great deal of what we write and say does not have a greater effect on us? The answer to that is complex, but one important aspect of it is the failure of motivational force in anything that gets too intellectualized. We are not moved totally as human beings by those phenomena that are directed to only a portion of our personality. Whatever is told mostly in intellectual terms or is directed only to our minds has already been abstracted from life. While this is necessary for some purposes of understanding and analysis, intellectualization can be carried to the point where it divorces even the most vital subject from the context of ordinary living. Love can thus be divested of its human trappings. It then emerges defused of its explosive possibilities, a cooled-down topic that can be approached more safely. You don't need tongs or asbestos gloves to pick it up and inspect it from various angles. Intellectualizing too much about a subject like love tones it down for us and wraps it in a defensive cover that marks it for the mind only. There is no stirring in the rest of us, no pressure on our innards to change ourselves or to be different in our dealing with people.

We do this to love and to other related subjects whose full meaning only comes clear when we open our total personalities to them. Faith and hope are classic examples of other values that we systematically eviscerate of their human fullness in order to deal with them in a more antiseptic intellectual way. A high price is exacted from us when, for fear of challenge or of being hurt, we deal with the most important values of life in a way that imposes distance between them and our own experience. Because we have indulged in overintellectualization for so many centuries we have gotten our human personalities badly out of focus. We have, for example, tended to idealize practically out of sight the elements that are most important for a fully human life. You only exaggerate things in an ideal manner when you have dealt too long with man in a totally intellectualized way. The idealized version of personal existence encourages man to believe that he is alive when he is only thinking vaguely beautiful thoughts about being alive. This approach also makes the ideals of life virtually unattainable by men who can still feel the wounds of their own humanity a thousand times a day.

Life does not take place on that cold and starlit intellectual plain. Life is lived on a very different, far from ideal level where even the best of men make big mistakes in the daily pursuit of their fullest humanity. Man is engaged in a process of growth, and while he needs ideals about such things as hoping and loving, these must not be so distant as to be totally beyond him. One of the worst failures of the institutions, such as the Churches and the universities, which are meant to help man, is their estrangement from the ordinary experience of imperfect men. Professors and theologians necessarily reflect on life in an intellectual way. The problem arises when they forget that hardly anybody else can handle life very effectively on that level. Politicians, at least, have a feeling for the disordered state of human affairs and for the strategies that work in getting things done. Somewhere between the impossibly ideal world of the scholar and the sometimes cynical real world of the politician is the territory where most men live.

We live, as a matter of fact, in an age of reaction to the overintellectualization of life. Anthropologists and other observers have been reminding man in books like *The Naked Ape* and *On Aggression* of his animal inheritance and the damage he does to himself when he forgets it. Man is not just intellect, they seem to be saying, and his planning and theorizing take him only so far. There are limitations and conditions to life—a body, feelings—that are also man. Man struggling to rediscover his unity and to achieve some of the wholeness that comes when everything that he is, mind and body, intellect and emotions, fit together. Man wants, in other words, to get back into relationship with himself, to take up the friendship that is fundamental to all others.

There is something more touching than offensive about his present symbolic and anti-rational struggles to lay hold of relationship to himself again. His protests are fragmentary and half-formed at times and as varied as only things man does can be. At one moment he is man the infantile and narcissistic; at another, man the playful and poetic. The protest is, however, the same; down inside, man is groaning for something more than cold, clear knowledge, and for something better than liberation for his animal urges. He really wants something to match his deepest if garbled yearnings; he wants to experience, in all the aspects of his personality, the meaning of friendship and love.

Man wants this in a language he can understand, from those who show some signs of having experienced life as it is rather than as it might be in some ideal world. It is not an easy task or an easy time in which to take it up.

The Gospels, if they are about anything, concern love and man's efforts to learn how to love more deeply and more creatively. Beautiful words and glowing sermons may be as unreal for the average man as intellectual speculation about remote theological themes. But, as pioneer psychiatrist Otto Rank once said, "The only therapy is life." So, too, the only way to avoid intellectualizing love is to write from what you have learned about it in your own experience.

To speak about love in something other than stained-glass tones, you must face and deal with it as you have encountered it in your own life. What you say will not be perfect and will not fit all cases; it may lack a certain theological finesse, but it will at least be real. As such it represents human experience reaching out to other human experience. Shortcomings will be present, but there is a chance to make up for them by a real willingness to share what you have suffered yourself.

The problem of life is really the problem of love. Anybody who thinks otherwise has not really faced much of life yet. Everywhere I go, I see lonely people who, even though they cannot put their longing into words, are still hoping for some experience of love and understanding that will give them the strength to face life with a little more courage. As the narrator of Thornton Wilder's *Our Town* noted, "You knows' well as I do: people are never able to say right out what they think of money, or death, or fame, or marriage. You've got to catch it between the lines; you've got to *over*-hear it." Of man's longing and loneliness, there is much to be overheard. What you can hear tells you how much people need and want the substance and direction that only real love brings into life.

People really are not looking for somebody with all the answers for life's riddles; they are quite prepared to live with mystery when the sustaining power of love is present. Neither do people expect that some new messiah will reveal to them the complete meaning of life. They look rather for something that will give them the strength to bear with life even when its meaning is obscure and its pressures are intense. They don't want fairy-tale happy endings as much as the chance to get into life more deeply and to love each other more truly. They can accept the seeming unfairness of life, with all its pains and disappointments, when they have been touched by love, and when they have learned that sharing love and friendship is what holds life together. The saints and wise men, by whatever other title we call them, have been friends to man and have helped other people to love each other a little more.

I am in a somewhat curious position in writing about the difficulties of loving. Some people within the Church have been critical of me precisely because I have written and spoken about love before. They would be more comfortable if I did not write about it or if I always made careful distinctions between the love of God (good) and the love of one's fellow man (less good) or woman (highly suspect). Well, I do not believe that you can successfully set Divine and human love over against each other, as though they were antagonistic elements. Real love is all of one piece, and the man who does not face and deal with the human love that comes to him in life has little chance of understanding God's love. You do not give up the one to achieve the other. A man confronts his responsibility toward the person he loves, and in carrying this out faithfully he begins to understand something about the God who is love. Love has its own discipline and demands that are unknown to people who flee from it.

I am not writing this to answer my critics as much as to carry out the responsibilities that experiencing real love in life has placed upon me. You need not be married to sense the pressure in real love to share as best you can what you have learned about life from loving and being loved. When you have experienced real love you know that it does not come in any ideal state, that it is marked with pain as well as joy, and that, if you are serious about it, you have to keep growing in it and working at it. You also know that you cannot keep the experience of love for yourself, that you have to give it away as freely as you have received it, in something of the spirit with which Paul Tillich wrote, "We only want to show you something we have seen and to tell you something we have heard."

That is how I feel about this book. It casts a vote for man and his possibilities when he can be opened to the source of all love, God Himself. But that love is worked out, not on the mountaintop of retreat, but in the everyday round where lovers find the real meaning of life. What is said in this book can only be a partial picture of the challenges of friendship and love. I know that wherever I can honestly share my own experience I have a chance of reaching others in a human and helpful way. That is what I think I am, as a preacher of the Gospel, asked to do by the Spirit who is the source of all the love any of us ever know.

EUGENE C. KENNEDY
F.S.

WHAT DO PEOPLE DO ALL DAY?

> Once I remember in London
> how I saw
> Pale shabby people standing in a
> long
> Line in the twilight and the misty
> rain
> To pay their tax. I then saw
> England plain.
>
> —Alice Duer Miller

Man makes you cry if you look at him long enough. That is the difficult part, to keep a steady gaze at all that goes into every human life. Because a real look at man's life becomes almost unbearably painful, each age creates an escape for itself. Black humor, for example, is a chilling refuge from the stress of life. So, too, a new supercool cynicism defends men against the suffering of being alive by making a huge put-on of everything to which man has attached meaning and value. It then demands, in the coolest commitment of all, faith in the put-on. If it is all make-believe it can never really hurt you. These are but two of the varieties of games men play when seeing man as he really is becomes too personally involving and painful.

Man's life is quite homely and strikingly beautiful, ordinary and unusual, full of vanity and yet profoundly moving, all at the same time. One of the most touching questions that can be asked about man concerns what goes on in the major parts of his life, what, if you will, he does all day. The truth is that the average man does not do very

much that seems exceptional. He does, in fact, pretty
much the same things from day to day. Call it rut or routine, it is nonetheless the path of life for most people. The
extraordinary meaning of everyday life lies hidden from
our usual glances, much as does pop art and found poetry.
It is only as we look afresh at it that we begin to understand its majesty as the setting in which people find and
love each other.

Even if the "average man" of the statistician does not
exist, average men abound and it is in their comings and
goings, their dreams and their longings, that we discover
the texture of life in the human condition. It is interesting
to note how little we seem to know from a psychological
viewpoint about the normal person. Even that research
which has been done on normality has been carried out
largely on college students, rather than on a more repre-
sentative group of the population. The ordinary man, cop-
ing as best he can with the pressures of life, remains a
shadowy figure, but he is most of mankind.

Much of what psychology and psychiatry tell us about
man comes from the study of abnormality and from clinical experience with people whose disorders are painful
enough to drive them into doctors' offices. But that is not
all of man either, and it is hardly a definition of the normal
person to describe him as not having any psychiatric symptoms.

It has been remarked before that although we have
many categories to describe mental illness (nine kinds of
schizophrenia, for example) we have very few terms, outside of "normal" and "healthy" to describe the soundness
of man. There is a message about the wonder of the ordinary in this. When persons suffer mental illness, they lose
something of their individuality insofar as they exhibit
common kinds of behavior that we call symptoms. Because of the similarity of their symptoms, people can be

classified as having the same kind of illness. That is not the way with the ordinary healthy person, however. Healthy people cannot be put into categories for a startlingly simple reason. They are all different from one another. Health manifests itself in the unique qualities of each person; this gives us a sense of the richness and the diversity of the human race. When you sense the differences of personality in lives that seem so much the same it is difficult to describe mankind with the slate-gray term, "the masses."

Mankind has never lacked people with convictions about how other people should behave. Codes of behavior and ideals of conduct have been, for example, a part of organized religion since the first sunrise. It is strange indeed that Churchmen have too often failed to have a feeling for the average struggling person. If they had, they would not have imposed the unattainable ideals they have at times presented as appropriate for human beings. They would have been more friendly, more compassionate toward man the mistake-maker. Indeed, the popular vision of the preacher as a somewhat stiff, proper, and slightly inhuman second lead in the drama of life makes him quite estranged from the forgiving and loving Christ of the Gospels. Of course, it has not been just religion that has proposed overidealized roles for men: The educator's dream of perfectible man, the chauvinist's vision of a master race; these die hard and slowly in history. Do-gooders have suffered from the occupational hazard of expecting more from man than he can ordinarily give. That tends to disappoint the do-gooders and to make men feel neurotically guilty about being human.

A good look at man in general makes us more sympathetic to the fallible condition of men in particular. To see and understand men as they are is the only way to avoid the cynicism and the heartlessness that plague those who expect more from man than he can deliver. When

you view the panorama of human growth you cannot help
but notice how flawed it is. It is anything but a smooth
and graceful curve arching upward and forward through
the time and space of history. There are rather sharp de-
clines, retraced pathways, graph lines bulging like aneu-
rysms, and even gaps at times. Man is faulted, and each
man tells the tale in a different way in his own life. The
remarkable thing is the extraordinary achievement of the
human species when the odds have been so high against
it. The touching thing is that imperfect men are capable
of the most profound experiences that we can know; they
can love and trust, have hope and be faithful to one
another. Yet these most tender experiences are found only
in humans and always in a manner that is imperfect. That
is one of the things you notice if you look to see what
people do all day. They pass from one incomplete experience to another, always unfinished themselves, and always
searching for the friendship and love that make them
grow. All this goes on in simple ways that are cruelly
tied to the limiting dimensions of the passing of time
and the shifting of circumstances.

Few men experience very often what psychologist
Abraham Maslow has described as the "peak moments"
of life. Even those who are models of maturity carry
barely healed scars that remind them of their fallibility.
The ordinary man pursues wholeness, but he never closes
the gap that separates him from it. Life is just not marked
with many first-class performances. Great achievement be-
longs to a relatively few men in each age; great adventure
to not many more; a constant sense of the romance of
living to hardly any at all. We lack a fully developed picture of the striving for life that is characteristic of most
people. We either write man off as an animal whose good
luck has brought him a long way in evolution, or we expect that he will act like an angel. Neither of these, of

course, is man as we really find him in his everyday life. We have not, in other words, sensitized ourselves to man the common, man the humanly understandable, man the incomplete who yearns for fulfillment.

What do people do all day? The answer must reflect the very ordinary things which go into the whole process of human growth. Most people do not, in one sense, do much on any day. They rise and wash and feed their families; they edge their way through the traffic to their jobs or stay home and do the housework; they pay their bills and go back into debt; they go to school, daydream, watch television, and wait for tomorrow. Life, as predictably dull as it sounds, is filled with the little human mysteries that mark man's way with things. These events, as simple as a husband's smile at coming home to his wife and children in the evening, make something magic out of things that seem so simple. The round of life, full of waiting and planning and worrying, is the setting for men to share life with each other. It is in the plain places of life that man experiences his most precious moments. The times of exchanging trust and giving hope, the ever-wondrous moments of entering into love with each other, the sense of really being present to one another: These are what hold life together and bridge the days that seem so much the same.

What is really important in life underlies rather than overwhelms the routine of living. Love and trust in action always look commonplace and undramatic. There is no grand exaltation that is experienced in the ordinary moments of life. Yet it is during these ordinary moments that we are fulfilled by each other's love. There are, of course, great and appropriate moments of celebration, feasts when we rightly put our most important relationships into focus. Anniversaries and birthdays bring us together for heightened moments of understanding how we really feel about each other. Grief and illness do the same thing in a different way. These moments of greater sensitivity to each other, of realizing how much we count on and care for each other, come, by common judgment, too rarely and pass swiftly by. Most men do not realize the profound meaning of the long days of life until they are passed. That is why in most of the research on what people remember as the happiest period of their lives, the time of just getting started, the period when so much is learned in such a hard way, usually finishes far ahead of any later time of achievement. It is in the great unself-conscious times of growing together through sharing what seems so routine that people are really alive to one another. That is why these people have something to celebrate when they worship on Sunday or when a birthday or anniversary rolls around. That is why they can enjoy doing things that seem so simple together, the richness that they have quietly built up through all the daily experience of really being in relationship to one another. And there is nothing sadder than the person who is so immature that he can never really be a part of everyday life with other persons. For persons like this, life only comes in the limelight, in the determined gaiety of parties and conversations where people hardly know each other. They think that life comes out of celebration when actually the only celebrations that ever mean anything come out of life itself.

There is something mysterious about the commonplace ways in which most people go through life. What, we might ask, are they looking for, except to do their best, to love each other, and to leave things better for their children? They search for the values that make life worthwhile, and they only find these when they can embrace the common settings of life completely. They then discover the very great difficulty that is involved in everyday living, the far excursions and testing of the human spirit that go with the basic relationships of loving and believing in others. Man discovers, when he allows himself to become a part of real life, the pain of being human.

This pain has nothing to do with sickness or with mankind's sometime savagery. It is rather the suffering of the healthy person, pain with a thousand private faces, the pain that goes with the vulnerability of just being alive. No man is inoculated against the ache of his struggle to become himself as a human being and a child of God. Money cannot buy it off, luxuries do not soften it, and no jet plane travels far or fast enough to outdistance it.

Man cannot run away from this pain without running away from himself. He can narcotize himself in a hundred ways against it, but he thereby numbs himself to the very deepest meaning of life. Man can only face and deal with it honestly. In facing the normal pain of life a man discovers his own inner strength to be free and responsible. His best self begins to emerge when he confronts the truth about his inescapable limitations and longings. This happens whenever a person senses the ragged boundaries of the human condition as set in space and time. He faces it whenever he wonders, in whatever situation, whether he can make it or not. Indeed, it is the quite ordinary effort to believe in oneself and in others that makes men recognize each other as brothers.

The twinges of life are most keenly experienced in our relationships with each other. We feel them in moments of misunderstanding, in the uneasy times, for example, when a friend demands a loyalty which would make us untrue to ourselves. We feel it when we cannot seem to break through to another and are left alone with some personal grief. Pain is present when we face freedom's choices and we are not at all sure what the right course will be either for ourselves or for others. Pain is always a possibility in love and friendship because it is in these ex-

periences that we are challenged to trust others even when
we are afraid to do it.

What life is really all about flows from the simple experience of what we are like with those we love. There
is no life except in relationship to others, be they spouses,
friends, children, or pupils. Lovers, who have discovered
the only experience that transcends time and space, know
a lot about suffering. If they have not tasted the pain of
loving, they are not really lovers at all. Even those who
love most deeply know the suffering that is sown into all
love. There are separations and good-bys, the tests of
growing old and staying in love, the challenges to be faithful and responsible to each other even as life alters them
and their circumstances. What nourishes the love of a man
and woman long after they have had to face the truth about
each other's failings and the truth about the commonplace nature of much of their life together? Lovers find
faith and hope only when they have faced pain together,
the pain that is never completely dulled, the pain that
is not an impurity but an essential part of the precious
metal of love.

This pain is part of every lover's longing, not diminished
but rather heightened by the realization that, in this life,
lovers can never share each other or anything else completely. So they rely on each other in a trial of faith and
trust that is never over and done with. They understand
hope because they constantly make themselves vulnerable
through believing in one another. Real lovers never escape
the pain of life, but they do conquer the restlessness that
betrays the unloving and the unloved. They find peace
and it passes all understanding, because they realize how
much dying goes into everyday living.

There is a great deal of talk about the risk involved in
loving. This is not, however, a risk that means the outcome will be either painful or pleasurable for us. Suffering

is, in fact, guaranteed for anyone who takes on the task of loving. The man who loves will suffer, but he will also find a fullness of life and a personal experience of the Spirit's presence. "What the Spirit brings," St. Paul wrote to the Galatians, "is very different" from the tangled emotions that the self-indulgent inherit. The Spirit brings "love, joy, peace, patience, kindness, goodness, trustfulness, gentleness and self-control." These are, of course, all virtues that describe our relationships with each other, the fruits of committing ourselves to the ordinary struggle to love. Outside of sharing life with each other in a thousand simple ways, there is no setting in which these can mean anything.

There is a terrible beauty about life that we all try to grasp and hold on to. We want to deal with the questions of life and love and even death itself. And it all takes place during the everyday give and take when we do not seem to be doing anything very special, but when we are actually deep within the heart of life itself. We get a hint of the wonder of our common experience from time to time. It may strike us so strongly that we reach out to grab a moment of happiness, only to find that it slips quickly and forever away. Something of that is caught in *Our Town* when Emily wants to go back to life for a day. She will pick a happy day, she says, but the stage manager warns her, "You not only live it; but you watch yourself living it. . . . And as you watch it, you see the thing that they—down there—never know. You see the future. You know what's going to happen afterwards." But Emily must go back, and so she chooses her twelfth birthday. But it is indeed filled with pain, the pain of seeing how important the everyday meaning of life is and of how little this is realized during the moments we live it. Emily speaks into the re-created past that cannot hear her; "Oh, Mama, just look at me one minute as though you really saw me.

Mama, fourteen years have gone by. I'm dead. You're a grandmother . . . Wally's dead too—We just felt terrible about it—don't you remember? But, just for a moment now we're all together. Mama, just for a moment we're happy. Let's look at one another. . . . I can't. I can't go on. Oh! Oh! It goes too fast. We don't have time to look at one another. I didn't realize . . . all that was going on and we never noticed."

Emily goes back to her grave, overwhelmed by realizing the richness of life that is taken so much for granted during the ordinary living of it. Nobody can try to press people for a more self-conscious mode of living than is normal or natural. And yet, the person who cannot see into the heart of his ordinary life experience is impoverished indeed. There is not much hope that he will ever understand the small miracles of living that are generated by the big miracle of people who face life with little to protect themselves but faith and hope and love for each other. The question cannot really be "What do people do all day?" It comes down to who they are to each other all day. It is through this basic presence to each other that human beings find the meaning of life and the fullness of life God wants them to share. It is in all that goes into reaching and getting closer to each other against a thousand simple backdrops that we redeem each other. There is no way to make a larger meaning out of life for the man who has missed the meaning of friendship and love. These are the great realities of human experience that give meaning to the rest of life. "Oh, earth," Emily says in a great Christian affirmation of what really counts, "you're too wonderful for anybody to realize you. Do any human beings ever realize life while they live it—every, every minute?"

ESTRANGEMENT FROM FRIENDSHIP

Man, made to find himself in all that is familiar, seems tragically lonely. It is as though he has turned away from the everyday scenes where the real values of life are to be found and has wandered, like the prodigal son in the Gospels, "to a far country" in search of them. He has tried to make his loneliness less painful through a wide variety of explorations in sex, alcohol, and drugs. Despite all this, his loneliness will not go away. It is a ghost looking back at him from his own mirror, a specter waiting for him around the corner of his next effort to escape it. Not everybody laughs these days, but everybody recognizes the iron-cold grip of loneliness on the human heart.

Men are lonely for different reasons and in different ways. It comes as the deep and brooding withdrawal of the mentally ill whose own dark and fearful worlds open painfully if at all to the approach of friends. Sometimes loneliness comes as the aching void in a family when one of its loved ones dies. So, too, there is the loneliness of the man who knows more than his comrades and thereby becomes a prophet, not only without honor but without friends as well. There is the loneliness of the person who is misunderstood and who cannot seem to communicate his real feelings to others. And there is the loneliness that creative people must find and face if they are to share their vision of the world with other men. There is a loneliness that goes with waiting, and life seems to be filled with waiting for so many people. It is the daily round for the housewife, waiting for the children, waiting for her husband, waiting in doctors' offices, outside schools, and beside railroad stations. It is a loneliness of expectation and a loneliness of drudgery, and it is as common as the rain.

There is even a special loneliness for lovers, for those who know most intimately the joys of sharing their life and struggles together. This comes at the many times when they must be apart, or in the moments when they realize how much they want to share and how limited they are in ever sharing completely the best of things in the human condition. Real lovers are not lonely because they are unloved; they know the unique mystery of separation that is heightened precisely because they are loved deeply. "Loneliness," Thomas Wolfe once wrote, "far from being a rare and curious phenomenon, peculiar to myself and to a few other solitary men, is the central and inevitable fact of human existence." There is something in loneliness that helps men to recognize each other as brothers in the human family. This is because it is such a common experience, one that we all know very well.

Loneliness has many faces, but the ache in the heart is the same for each one of them. Each man seems to feel it, and to find himself pressed enough to catch a glimpse of what Bertrand Russell in his autobiography called "that terrible loneliness in which one shivering consciousness looks over the rim of the world into the cold lifeless abyss." Men can feel so terribly alone that they are estranged from friendship, from that one thing that can rescue them from the isolation and the emptiness that fill life when there is no love in it. Contemporary man is suffering a friendship deprivation with effects that are just as drastic and just as harmful as the deprivation of air, water, or food would be. Where he is not totally deprived, he is suffering from a problem of social pollution which darkens his environment and makes it hard for him to breathe and stay alive with his fellow men.

The American landscape is filled with the evidence of man's loneliness and his attempts to cope in some way or other with it. It is streaked with paradox; men feeling more alone in the midst of a population explosion; men feeling empty inside in the midst of affluence; men feeling cut off in the age of communication. Ordinary people are under the stress that is imposed on them because of their enterprise and invention. Man's mobility allows him to travel as never before, and yet it makes it more difficult for him to set down roots in any community. It is harder then for him to find the kind of consistently supportive relationships that usually last a man a lifetime.

The family itself is under pressure especially as the age of the extended family comes to a close. The family unit is more self-contained, and its members no longer have the emotional support of many close relations living with or near them. Husband and wife tax each other to satisfy each other's emotional needs with greater intensity than in the past. There has been a cultural shift in our way of looking at and expecting things from marriage. In previous eras marriage was emphasized as an institution necessary for the preservation of the race and the good of society. The relationship of the couples was somewhat secondary; they did not expect so much from each other, and there was not so much disappointment if the emotional aspects of marriage were not completely fulfilling. Now, however, marriage is perceived primarily as a personal relationship and only secondarily as an institution. Man and woman have much higher expectations about the relationship and are much more disappointed when it is not as idyllic as they had hoped. Marriage as an institution is under consequent stress, as one can tell from the divorce statistics. But the loneliness lies beneath the statistics, in the couples made wary of the intimacy they still seek by the wounds of their experience of marriage. Loneliness is multiplied

again in the lives of the children who have seen the only
world of human relationship they know fall apart around
them.

We also live in the age in which man's loneliness and
alienation have been identified as something like a national
epidemic. Psychology and psychiatry have responded with
variations on the theme of group dynamics. The age of
Aquarius is also the age of sensitivity training and encounter groups, which have been described by psychologist
Carl Rogers as "the most important social invention of
this century." The very presence of this kind of response on
a massive scale throughout the country is a clear indication
of the proportions of the problem of modern man's estrangement from friendship. In these groups men have
learned to weep for their isolation from each other. They
have, in other words, broken the shell of the overintel-
lectualized version of life and have moved into a fuller
and freer expression of their feelings. Often enough in
the experience of these groups this expression of feeling
is set over against reason. Man's pain has driven him to
rediscover his feelings and to bring them to the surface
in his relationships with other group members. As is the
way with swinging pendulums, there have been many failures to integrate this newly liberated emotional side of
man with the rational and understanding aspects of his
personality.

Because of the rapid rise of various forms of group dynamics in response to man's estrangement, there have been
some serious problems with the unprofessional and manipulative activities of some persons associated with this
movement. While they have been repudiated by responsible professionals, they continue to operate. In their blundering manner they often open people up but fail to
follow through in helping these people to understand
themselves. They only add to the epic loneliness and es-

trangement of the age. Characteristic of these groups is the sudden flash explosion of long-smoldering anger in its members. This is often the hostility built up through a lifetime of frustration in trying to reach and deal more humanly with others. Now the hatred spews out in an authenticity that is more destructive than life-giving. When people who do not understand what they are doing provoke this kind of behavior they often produce more long-range isolation than was present in the person's life before. So, too, the hand of the amateur can be seen in those groups where the members practically devour each other, as though the ingestion of another person would be productive of one's own identity. Sadly enough, the emergence of group dynamics attests to and sometimes complicates our contemporary loneliness. This may be because so many of these groups are too shortsighted as yet to see man in accurate perspective. They do not see man whole, nor do they see all of his needs. As Arthur Burton has noted:

Western man has reacted to his loneliness by a great spirit of group behavior and by an obsessive interest in group dynamics. Industry and business have become group centered. . . . despite the tremendous increase in "groupiness," the feelings of loneliness have kept pace with group growth and even outdistanced it. It was Jung who pointed out that, particularly in the United States, a child is deprived of the solitude necessary to find himself. (*Modern Humanistic Psychotherapy*, San Francisco, Jossey-Bass, Inc., 1967, pp. 42, 43)

There is a clue to modern man's estrangement from friendship in Burton's last observation. In many ways we have systematically denied ourselves the opportunity we need to discover our own personalities. This failure, for whatever reason, to come to terms with our own identity deprives us of the relationship to self that is the precondi-

tion for relationship with anyone else. Instead of sharing
their identity with another person, in itself a complicated
task, many persons look for their identity from others.
They tear at them, dig into them, depend like a dead
weight from them, until the relationship collapses under
the strain. Estrangement from friendship flows basically
from a primary estrangement from oneself.

A lot goes into making it possible for a person to meet
and deal in a healthy manner with his own self. The process of achieving individuality is not easy, and it requires
sensitivity and understanding on the part of parents and
teachers. Sadly enough, this process has been short-
circuited in our day because of many parents who have
had neither the insight nor the patience to help their children bring their own personalities into the light of day.
They have preferred to make their children over according
to their own needs or their own expectations. There is
considerable evidence that demonstrates the significant
role the parents play as the intermediaries between the
child and the larger world. Vital to this role is the care
with which parents mediate the child's growing awareness
of himself. When, because of their own needs or anxieties,
parents do violence to this process or distort it badly, they
contribute to the child's estrangement from the human
family in which he longs to live.

Examination of a few aspects of this problem makes
clear the complications that can arise when a person tries
to establish relationships with others before his relationship to himself is relatively secure. Many American parents
are more than mildly anxious about the social success of
their children. They want them to be popular, to be part
of whatever is fashionably "in" at the moment. This is not
only for the sake of the children but for the sake of the
parents, many of whom lead a vicarious social life through
the experiences of their children. These parents are often

the type who need desperately to be popular with their children as well; they want them to like them, and so they dread ever saying *no* to them. They have been conditioned by a generation of pop psychology to fear that every *no* may be the source of potential trauma for the children.

Actually, as psychoanalyst Ralph Greenson has observed, these parents have difficulty in even thinking that they might raise anger in their children. That is the response they dread, and the one they fend off with their elaborate permissiveness and efforts to please the children at all costs. Interestingly enough, such parents reveal more about themselves than they think. They make clear their own difficulty with loving relationships. As Greenson notes, "clinical experience has demonstrated that people who cannot cope with different varieties of hate, anger, and resentment, will also have trouble with different forms of love." (Ralph Greenson, M.D., "Sexual Apathy in the Male," *Medical Aspects of Human Sexuality*, August 1969.) The popularity-conscious parent who cannot face the anger of his own children fails to love them properly and offers them a poor model for their own imitation.

Beyond this, it is common for certain parents to push their children into dating experiences before the children are emotionally able to handle the experience. Here again, the need of the parent, the urgent anxiety that the child assume a successful heterosexual role as soon as possible in life, has forced the child into experiences for which his own maturity has not yet prepared him. This is complicated by the quite pervasive fear of homosexuality in America. This motivates parents to urge their children into heterosexual roles before the time is really right for them. There is a terrible uneasiness, perhaps some uncertainty in the parent's own sexual identification, that lies beneath this quite widespread phenomenon.

The result, often enough, is to deprive the young of the childhood and youth they are meant to enjoy. It is to transform what should be magical years of the exploration of the world and their own wonder at it into times of anxiety and pressure. Perhaps there is nothing more devastating to a person than to rob him of his youth. When this occurs, we take away the time and the kinds of experience a person needs to lay the groundwork for his own identity. For example, the anxiety to get a young boy or girl involved in heterosexual relationships may well cut out or distort a normal period of life in which it is perfectly healthy and vitally important for each of them to learn to make friendships with members of his own sex. Most students of human development have recognized the importance of this stage of growth as a significant step in beginning to understand the meaning of personal sharing with another human being. For parents to foreshorten their children's opportunities to understand friendship because of fear of homosexuality and the desire for social success is to estrange them from the meaning of friendship.

If we try to understand the protests of modern youth we will see a symbolic acting out of their estrangement from friendship, and their uneasiness at being forced into relationships of intimacy before they are ready for them. These protests are prophetic, not clearly understood by youth and yet with a message for the adult world. It seems quite likely that the boy-girl pairs who dress alike and wear their hair at the same length are trying to tell us something. They are saying that they are uneasy with sexual differences and so they try to obscure them rather than sharpen them. They tell us that they are not looking for a lover who is different from them but for a friend who is almost exactly like them. They are trying to control their own anxiety at being expected to take on mature heterosexual roles by reverting to the friendship period that was denied to so many of them during their earlier years. They are, as Greenson has observed, looking for a twin rather than a sweetheart, telegraphing to us the message that they feel secure with someone who resembles themselves, that they are compensating for the friendship they missed while growing up.

This explains a good deal of the exploratory nature of relationships among young people, their emphasis on openness and some form of community, their feeling of solidarity against the adult world, and the amazing absence of much really rich sexual experience in these relationships. They act like tentative friends with secret signs and passwords, prizing each other and yet fearful of the loss of each other. In many ways these young people are simply acting out the experiences which they never had in much depth at the age when they should have. Their interest in the unisex styles is clear evidence of their ambivalent feelings about adult sexuality where the differences between men and women make for excitement and fascination. There is something forlorn about many of these young people who are trying to rediscover the meaning of friendship in a culture that has despoiled them of a vital part of their lives.

Our culture offers other urgings, of course, connected with human relationships, many of which have equally harmful effects on the individual's capacity to form mature and loving relationships. There is, for example, the widespread pressure for premarital sex. Here again, something rich and essential to full growth—establishing a responsible and caring relationship for another—is shunted aside in favor of sexual pleasure that is thereby drained of much of its meaning. We have gone a long way to separate sex from love in this era of loudly heralded sexual liberation. Indeed, with dispiriting and pathetic consequences, we have justified and made available immediate gratification in the area of sexual expression. Disregarded are the ingredients that are always essential to any relationship of love that is meant to outlast the moment. There is never any need to put up with frustration or separation, no need to face the suffering and overcoming of obstacles that tests the strength of real love. Having dispensed with the need to struggle and endure, the young are really denied an understanding of the elements that have been a part of deep and romantic love for as long as men can remember. They are thus estranged, as are many of their parents, from love and friendship in another way.

To enjoy sex together may offer some pleasure to young people, but it is also a way to cut off rather than to enter into relationship with each other. This means death to love and friendship in the long run. In the short run it often leads to disappointment with sex because, lacking the expressive power of a real human relationship, sex can be drab and mean. It is no wonder that so many of the young turn to the artificial stimulation of drugs; they are seeking the warmth and color that are not provided by their own thin and tenuous relationships with each other. It is, after all, difficult to kindle any real warmth when one has opted for coolness. In love and friendship coolness is a detaching and protective stance. It endorses pleasure, diversify it as you will, but it cuts off anything that means real human exchange.

Because of these and other forces that will be discussed later on, modern man is indeed a lonely and searching being. He is estranged from friendship and thereby disenfranchised from love. His new-found freedom and sophistication are all too often only the occasion for him to act out his own slavery to a primitive and undeveloped self. In the midst of the turmoil and confusion of the age, men are grabbing for identity outside themselves because they have failed to grow to their own fullness. All the madness and immaturity only heighten man's estrangement from even the beginnings of friendship to himself or the rest of mankind.

LIFE IS ALL ABOUT
MEN AND WOMEN

A large part of what Camus described as the "implacable grandeur" of this life arises from the mystery of man and woman. Life itself, not just romance, pivots on this fundamental relationship. It is in the meeting of man and woman that the full energies of humanity are brought together, not just for love-making, but as the fundamental pattern of the creative meaning of life itself.

We live, however, in a strange age in which anyone who suggests that heterosexuality is a relatively normal life style is suspected of an ancient and naïve bias. Present-day prophets tell us that Prometheus is already unbound, that "whatever turns you on" is a sufficient rule of thumb for life in the sexual open housing of a new era. Heterosexuality is a hangup, according to this liberated world view which claims that you can see man clearer if you see him blurred.

Indeed, this may well be the age of the blur in practically everything. Cheers still echo in football's Super Bowl when baseball's preseason practice has already begun. The pennant is still being contested and there is a sudden midsummer epiphany of football again. The other sports let their energies flow in and around these national pastimes like errant lubricants in the machinery of our diversions. The seasons of sports have ragged and runny edges, in a strange unconscious symbol of our affinity for the blur. The same can be said of other minor cultural characters, such as the villains on television. Perhaps it is sensitivity to the feelings of national subgroups that dictates this. It may, however, be the urge to blur that gives the bland and genealogically obscure names like Trask, Hance, and Bant to contemporary bad men. These neutral sounds are merely minor footnotes in the over-all cultural trend that blurs our understanding of man and woman.

There is no doubt that the battle to gain some kind of long-deferred equality for women has been a strenuous one. Men have found it difficult to accept women as full partners in human nature. The prejudice which has subjugated and denied rights and opportunities to women is one of history's oldest evils. One does not have to erase the differences between the sexes, however, to recognize the equality of woman's humanity. To cast aside the sentimental analogy of man as head and woman as heart, to retire the conviction that woman is the perennial domestic: These are not the same as to make woman into man in such fashion as to diffuse their separate identities and to end up with some neuter all-purpose person for the future.

Men and women are splendidly different even though they are rightfully equal. The wonder really is that they can live and work together at all. The fact that they are different is a revelation of the fullness of human nature. It also points to the vital elements that give life and movement to the story of mankind. The sources of the human race's progressive energies are the contrasting ones of man and woman. Polarity and equality are compatible truths about men and women.

Contrast and conflict between the sexes is neither surprising nor disturbing. Without them life would be a neutral and completely uncharming compromise. The fact is that life takes on pace and vigor precisely as man and woman can meet, take the measure of each other, and begin to know and love each other. This applies to a broader set of relationships than just courtship and marriage. It is only in the meeting of an authentic man and an authentic woman that the polarities of the human condition can be stimulated and co-ordinated. It is in the relationship of the sexes that the strength of each is thoroughly developed. The real powers of human nature are mustered whenever man and woman encounter each other.

There is an exciting tension between the sexes that is essential to the full development of each. This con-natural tension, which may be the sign of a thousand nameless conflicts, is not something to be anesthetized. It is the breath and blood of the drama of human creativity which is renewed in any real sharing of man and woman together. They begin to reveal themselves to one another, not in the oversimplified eroticism of instant intimacy, but in the joint learning together of the basic meaning of trust. It is the many-layered aspects of the self that are shared in the meeting of man and woman. It is because they can learn to love and trust one another that they can begin to talk the same language about the meaning of life.

The remarkable possibilities of human relationship are revealed in that of man and woman precisely because they are different from one another. This is not to deny the masculine and feminine elements which blend within any genuine man and woman. It is to recognize that the male and female elements within them have different centers of gravity. This clear identity within the person leads him to the promise and the challenge of sharing with others. A real man and a real woman, in other words, bring to each other a distinctive blend of the elements of humanity. It is in meeting each other that these contrasting blends are necessarily and constructively counterpointed. This does not happen, no matter what off-Broadway tells you, in any relationship of man to man or woman to woman in the same way.

It is in this opportunity for man and woman to begin to know each other that the conflicting antagonisms of their personalities can be overcome. Sparks may fly—and they will continue, in one way or another, to fly throughout their relationship—but this is because a subtle and quite complicated conflict must occur if the relationship of man and woman is to be creative. Creativity depends, in the understanding of modern research, on the presence of opposite trends and feelings within the creator, whether he is an artist, a writer, or a poet. The full force of these struggling energies is utilized without the obliteration of any of them. There is, then, in the act of creation some tense interaction between opposed psychological forces. The one-sided man does not create because he has not tolerated the ambiguity of feelings which is the condition for creativity. Something new comes into existence in the creative response because opposing energies have been tapped but not confused with each other.

So it is in the relationship of man and woman. There are differing elements which can come into creative relationship to one another. The price of creativity in the relationship will be the struggle for some genuine meeting between the person who is the man and the person who is the woman. They are not asked to negotiate a truce, or to make war under the banners that demand the unconditional surrender of the one or the other. Theirs is the opportunity for the sharing of their differences in such a way that their distinctive strengths are preserved and ordered toward the creation of something new. Generativity is the inherent potential of the meeting of man and woman.

This cannot be thought of solely in terms of their begetting new life in children. This is obviously important, but it is only one aspect of the over-all creative interrelationship of man and woman. Children, after all, can be begotten in strangely non-creative ways, in relationships which have not been the fusion of strengths of personality as much as the random and thoughtless fusion of biology.

Such children suffer often from the fact that their life came from something quite different than a rich and loving personal relationship of a genuine man and a genuine woman. They are neither conceived nor cared for in the atmosphere of continuing trust that is essential to the real meeting of man and woman in marriage. Life has something left out right at the start for these children, something that will inevitably manifest itself in their later emotional history.

The meeting of man and woman, neither sacrificing identity, is an essential but hardly simple fundamental aspect of all of life. It is because they possess separate clear identities which harmonize under the integrating force of love that they can give new life in a variety of ways to humankind. It is also in relationship to one another that man and woman are able to preserve their separateness from one another. This is one of the hallmarks of creative love. Lovers do not melt into a molten lump of humanity that makes cooing sounds of togetherness. They can, in fact, achieve and preserve a fullness of their own personalities in relationship to one another. When they are in a healthy and creative relationship men and women can be remarkably and refreshingly different. In fact, this is precisely one of the effects of authentic creative love. Man and woman free unsuspected richnesses in each other that enable them to be fully themselves. They can pursue different careers or develop contrasting interests without threatening each other's identities or their relationship to one another. It is in the genuinely creative sharing of men and women that the attractive contrasts of charm and humor, the quintessential interplay of the sexes, are most manifest.

Much of this is put to death under the now fading rubric of togetherness with its stifling and sticky lock-step model of the man-woman relationship. Togetherness never guarantees the development of man and woman in relationship to one another. It tends to confound the elements, and to smother the conditions of trust and openness which are so essential to the generative presence of male and female with each other. Indeed, togetherness has generated a great deal of frustration with its corollaries of working at play and pulling together in all things. Much healthier is the outcome of the situation in which men and women are free to pull against one another, to reveal their remarkable differences rather than to obscure them in obedience to the house rules of supposedly jolly suburban life. It is in retaining and developing their differences, as a matter of fact, that they spontaneously can play at work with one another, that they can tolerate a quota of healthy conflict, that they can be separate persons who love and trust one another.

Love and trust permit conflict, they do not totally extinguish it. Couples who feel they must be sweetly cooperative may be denying one of the basic resources of their relationship, their real differences, from one another. Under the compulsion to be self-sacrificingly pleasant, they may suppress rather than sacrifice their real selves. This means that they keep their real selves out of relationship to one another because they feel their duty is to sweet mutual reasonableness. Anything too sweet becomes cloying after a while. So it is with couples who are literally so afraid to let their real personalities out that they never get to know or to deeply love one another. They may have avoided the sparks of conflict but only because they have never kindled the fire of real love.

It is no wonder that men and women like this can wake up someday to discover that they really have never known each other, they have been so busy being nice to each other that the polarities of their persons have never come into contact. They have never really dealt with the genuine problem of intimacy, and so they literally have never fully met or understood each other. They have never struggled with the opposing aspects of themselves, and so they have never truly become complementary in relationship to one another. The failure to fuse their strengths under the integrative impulse of genuine love has denied them any experience of true creativity together. These are the couples who are deeply lonely but who cover it up with a style of relationship which is ultimately barren and isolating.

It is no wonder that someday, perhaps after the children are all off to school or after financial security has been attained, after the struggle to survive has abated, that they discover, much to their anguish and surprise, that they have no communication with each other. They have really never worked at the essential quality of the man-woman relationship, the common life of two separate persons. Indeed, they may have noted the symptoms of the fact that their real selves, despite the engagement ring, never became engaged with one another. Their sex life may have lost its magic, or may never have recovered from initial disappointments, even though they desperately tried to perform adequately according to all the manuals and cultural urgings. This is ultimately a disillusioning and destructive kind of relationship because the two persons have never met on the level of their contrasting identities.

Indeed, this is one of the root difficulties in many marriages, even where the enthusiasm for togetherness has not been awkwardly invoked in the name of genuine relationship. When persons approach a relationship, whether it is in friendship or marriage, without having worked out their own separate identities, then it is very difficult for them ever to share anything in a substantial way. They use the relationship, even though unconsciously, to find rather than to share their personal identities. This is not to deny that true friendship between man and woman will obviously enhance their individual self-definitions. This only occurs, however, if man and woman bring some adequate self-understandings to the relationship in the first place. If they do not, then there is only some protoplasmic self flowing in and around another amorphous self. Whether they like it or not, they then tend to try to make their identities out of the union in which they should, in fact, be correlating the strengths of their identities. They battle with each other because the prize is not creative union as much as individual reassurance as to their masculinity or femininity.

That is why there is so much genital combat, so much using of sex in a competitive and literally self-seeking way. The unconscious determinant of the struggle lies in the somewhat old-fashioned notion of selfishness. The logistics of a military campaign are quite naturally appropriate to describe the results. The conquest of the other is more important than the commitment to one another. That is why there is so much defensiveness in these relationships, and why some households seem sometimes to be armed camps with guards, early-warning systems, and quick escalation to all-out war. Every interaction, even the most casual, becomes the focus for some kind of war game, such as those described by Eric Berne. The secret of a successful marriage, however, is not in the mastery of these games or tactics, but in understanding why such a military turn of events should have come about in the first place. These people feel trapped, and so they describe their relationship as one full of secret snares. It is in this kind of embattled standoff that the persons can leave their flanks undefended. They are then vulnerable to other affairs or liaisons which seem to offer them what their own failed marriages have not provided. They have little understanding of the aggression which they use so much on each other.

Intimacy is a task of life which goes beyond but clearly includes sexual relationships. It is a challenge that can be safely accepted only by those who have a reasonable understanding and sense of freedom about their own identity. This means that intimacy, which binds people in creative sharing, is a life opportunity which can only be taken on by authentic men and women. It is not a proving ground as much as it is the setting for men and women to respond to each other in a genuinely loving way. Real love does not shackle people together. It rather frees them to be truly generative in relationship to one another. The achievement of identity that is substantial must precede this.

Freud's seemingly simple answer to the question of man's purpose in life is provocative as well as profound. He said that man was made "to love and to work." Genuine love that means the sharing rather than the searching for identity in relationship to the other necessarily is related to productivity. Freud did not mean that man was sentenced to drudgery. He suggested rather that man is called to be productive, to an authentic generativity that is associated with his capacity for love. He indicated that love and work are correlated human tasks. Man fails himself when his productive potential is so smothered in competitive achievement that he can no longer be, as psychoanalyst Erik Erikson has observed, "a sexual and loving being." Man cannot, in other words, survive or grow by working at love, in the anguished and uncomfortable manner which is so common in the relationships of those people who do not yet possess their own identity. Not possessing themselves, they cannot give themselves in any free or loving way to another. They are numb to the possibilities of opening up their true personalities in relationship to another. They kill, in a sense, the deep possibilities of authentic productivity in each other. It is no accident when some men try to marry their jobs as a substitute for their relationships with their wives.

A culture which misemphasizes genital sexuality forecloses quickly the possibilities of man and woman relating in the true dimensions of their humanity. It weights genital sexuality to the breaking point. It makes it a battleground rather than a significant aspect of the authentic resolution of the polarities of man and woman. This shrinking of the horizon obscures the real task of friendship between the sexes. It obliterates its ultimate ordering to a productive life-sharing in which the opposing elements of masculinity and femininity are harmonized in love that truly creates. It robs mature sexuality of the meaning that it has as the focus and celebration of the love of separate individuals.

There is involved in this, then, a need to preserve our understanding of the differences between man and woman. If their relationship is immature when their separate identities are unachieved, then the creative potential of human love is threatened by a surrender to the philosophies that blur the fundamental identities of man and woman. This has serious implications for all the personal and social activities of man. One may rely on some reactive common sense of the race to set things right in our perception of man and woman, but, in view of the present cumulative forces of change, it might be risky to do this. If we are at the gates of a polymorphous paradise, it is obvious that there will be a restyling or at least a higher social tolerance for relationships which dilute the creative potential of the man-woman relationship. Society already looks more acceptantly toward premarital sex, homosexual partners, and the companionate marriage which does not

include children. It is obviously unwise to group all of
these together or to judge them in the same way. It is,
however, important to see the implications of a reordering
of society on the basis of a melded perception of the sexes.

This is so because the nature of the man-woman relationship has long-range consequences for the patterns of
all the institutions of man. If the primal source of generativity in man is somehow distorted or diffused, then the
whole meaning and value of the generative spirit is
changed in society. Marriage, the family, the social institutions designed to preserve and nourish the creative
thrust in man will be modified as a result. There is a great
deal at stake in understanding that life is indeed all about
men and women.

The fundamental sharing that the man-woman relationship demands leads to a real fullness of life which moves
men and women to be concerned with and responsible
for the interests of others. Generativity, as Erikson has
noted, "is primarily the concern for establishing and guid-
ing the next generation." When people can no longer invest themselves in others because of a failure to achieve
this generous openness, this sense of caring for others,
whether their own children or the needy of the race, they
may "begin to indulge themselves as if they were their own
—or one another's—one and only child." A stagnation of
spirit, an isolation from human values, can quickly follow.
This conjures up Winick's vision of desexualized society as
"a bitter, metallic existence" which "may simply not be
worth the price of enduring it." (Charles E. Winick, *The
New People*, New York, Pegasus, 1968, p. xl.)

The world is confronted at present with the threat of
overpopulation, and conscientious men are presenting the
case for planned parenthood. Much of their concern is for
the welfare of succeeding generations. The difficulty lies
in the fact that man must be imbued with basic human

values if he is to employ scientific methods of birth regulation in a manner that will truly serve the needs of man. This is a tricky area, since the developments in birth regulation allow men to control their generativity. It may be that in an effort to avoid overcrowding the planet, man may alter his understanding of the basic values of life and love. Birth control is effective, but it is perilously employed by men who have simply turned in on themselves in a negation of the expansive potential of mature love.

Birth-control pills, in other words, may make it easier for men to overlook the fact that their thoughtless use can do violence to something essential to the continuing journey of the human race. Pills will not cure human relationships nor will they necessarily resolve the marriage problems of modern man. Their widespread use, without a correlative understanding of the creative demands of human love, may obscure further the nature of the man-woman relationship. The planning can totally precede the parenthood and put to death the spontaneous and essential dynamics of the man-woman relationship. This is not necessarily the case, but there is little evidence that the motivation for, much less the consequences of, birth regulation have been plumbed very deeply. This obligation to prepare carefully for a world in which children can be adequately fed and educated cannot eclipse a necessary concern for the possible effects of birth control on man's understanding of himself.

While it is easy to speak of birth control as something which allows man and woman to nourish their love for one another through their sexual relationships, it is important to realize that love withers in a self-conscious and self-centered elimination of the spontaneity and risk that are necessary to the true understanding of human generativity. The world may only become colder and more alienated if men and women are not nourished by a sense of values that can truly sustain the core element of their creative love for one another.

It is, after all, the free vitality of men and women who entrust themselves and their energies to each other that is basic to the achievement of identity by their children. If indeed, this basic and somewhat mysterious relationship is subjected to the continuing pressures that de-emphasize the deeper values of personality while they accelerate the depersonalization of sexual activity, we may be entering an age of paneroticism. This would lead to a decline, as Marshall McLuhan has observed, in genuine sexuality because sex will have lost its authentic meaning in human relationships. This is not an impossibility in a world that already warms to the ethic of "whatever turns you on."

It would merely be platitudinous to remark about the orientation of our culture toward pleasure as an end rather than a by-product of life. Man, driven so long by guilt and fear concerning sex, has only recently validated enjoyment in life. The balance has tipped past the mid-point of reaction, however, and the pursuit of pleasure, of the subjective experience of gratification, is pervasive in our culture. The difficulty here, of course, is that pleasure as a commanding goal means that man has already taken a step back from commitment with another to something beyond the self. This hedonistic withdrawal is attested to in many ways from the cigarette advertising that promises "more pure pleasure" through the building market of auto-erotic literature, to the college student seeking "a high" through pot, beer, or electronically amplified music. This trend to invest energy in subjectively satisfying experience kills the spirit of true generativity that inheres in the union of love.

True lovers are not so conscious of seeking pleasure as they are of affording it to one another. Indeed, the impulse of love leads to an unconditional surrender of man and woman to each other. It is in this union that they lose consciousness of all the world except for each other. It is here that they can drop the mask of defenses, that their polarities can be overcome, that what is diverse and competitive yields to the unifying and freeing power of their love. There is powerful pleasure in this experience, but it flows from the near transcendent sharing of the persons of the lovers, not from the calculation of pleasure seeking.

Even here there is a great deal of learning for husbands and wives. Husbands are sometimes puzzled at the differential reactivity of their wives in love-making. There are here, as everywhere in marriage, constant demands on tenderness, patience, and understanding that infuse sexual relationships with a richer humanity. It is indeed the occasion for a deeper search of the self on the part of both man and woman if they are to offer the loving gift of themselves fully to each other. It is a difficult and delicate setting for the progressive fusion of all that is different about each of them. When pleasure is the only goal, the meaning of man and woman in relationship to each other as fully human beings is attenuated.

It is hard to write rules about sexual relationships, although this has not dissuaded generations of lip-licking authors. There is something about the lessons of love-making that resists codification. Too much that is human and significant gets lost in the process. The lessons of love are, in fact, some of the more profound lessons of life experience, and they have a significance that suffers when reduced to the tactics of "how to do it," that emphasizes performance, as though men and women were actors rather than human beings who love one another.

You can write scenarios, with proper cues for entrances and exits, for performers. You cannot do this for loving men and women without stifling the spontaneity of their

self-giving in sexual relationships. Here masks and meas-
ured movements are inappropriate. There is, after all, an
abandonment of the self, and all that is self-conscious, in
the full surrender of love. Only men and women who are
relatively sure of their own identities can commit themselves freely to the liberating experience of genital union.
It is a journey which has seemingly regressive and irrational
aspects to it, a journey in the strong tides of the deepest
human feeling. Only a sense of inner direction that comes
from their own personal identities guides the experience
for men and women to its fullness. Sexual union is, for the
genuine man and woman, a tumultuous manifestation of
all that is human in them. At its best it is a time when
they are never less actors or more fully themselves. Acting
and pretense eat away at the meaning of authentic sexuality. A blurring of the identities of man and woman destroys it and its creative thrust completely.

The perennial problem is clearly one of balance, the
human balance that is alive with the tension of two persons who are capable of sharing so much and so thoroughly
that they can remain maturely different from each other.
This balance of life is impossible when the sexes are
blurred and eroticism replaces sex. No culture can survive
in a very healthy or creative condition if it cashiers the
identities which remind us of just how profoundly life is
all about men and women.

WHY SHOULD THEY
KNOW THE WAY?

Youth is a time for learning about love. During these years of life we begin to sense and respond to the enormous mystery of each other. Youth provides the setting in which our identity is made firm enough to bear the weight of our reaching out to others in ways that go deeper than the games of childhood. In youth we get our first understanding of that essential core of friendship that is the real beginning of a more mature love. We discover that others have a special meaning for us and that we can, in turn, have a special meaning for them. Human sharing with all its terrors and rewards opens up for us.

A man needs time in which to investigate this new world of intimacy and responsibility. It cannot be successfully compressed into some cram course. No Project Headstart takes the place of the months and years that are necessary for a person to internalize the meaning of friendship and love. During these years, when an individual's development is not distorted by cultural pressures, a young man or woman can experiment with various personal relationships. There are pitfalls and difficulties, of course, as a young person tests the trustworthiness of his friendships. Friendship with one's own sex contributes to the fullness of personality which an individual brings to his first relationships with the opposite sex. At this time arise the anguish and distractions of first loves, "Dear John" letters, and regularly broken hearts. A wide range of relationships provides a rich interpersonal environment in which the young can try their identity out on each other in the special world of new-found intimacy. New adult figures also play important roles in the lives of the young at this time. These may be teachers, priests, or aunts and uncles. They provide a new frame of reference as well as fresh models for the young person to follow during the period when he is deciding on how he will spend his life. In the age when practically everything else can be digested or compressed in one way or another, there is no way to foreshorten these human developmental experiences successfully.

Unfortunately, in many ways this is exactly what we have done to young people during this century. We have robbed them of their youth and denied them the years and many of the opportunities which they need to deal with and to establish their own identity and to move toward the kind of maturity that is essential for the adult exchange of love. Observers tell us that there is a new life stage, one that intervenes between adolescence and adulthood, one with its own proper characteristics and problems, and that its name is youth. Because of the conditions of affluence, the extension of education, and the new patterns of engagement in the world of work, the young enjoy a leisure unknown to previous generations. In great numbers they are freed from the necessity of making an immediate decision about their life's work or of joining the labor force right after the end of schooling. Neither need they make a quick decision about marriage. These young people have money, mobility, and an increasing amount of influence on the tastes and choices of the rest of culture. They have flexed their political and cultural muscles, and the rest of the world has noticed. Indeed, there are those who say that youth is actively establishing a counterculture.

The observers of this new life stage are probably quite accurate in the way they describe it. There is a new plateau where a kind of preadult life is taking place. The problem is that at this life stage there are implicit demands on the young to act as if they had already left their youth long behind them, to present themselves as though they had completely achieved the identity which is indispensable to friendship and love.

There is a noble and idealistic ring to this new life stage of youth. It flies the banners that read "Despise hypocrisy and remake the world," its agenda is crowded with concerns for freedom and the human person, its objective a new society filled with peace and love. One can only be touched deeply by the sincerity of so many of the young, even as one realizes how much we are asking them to bear of the burdens of the world before they are fully grown themselves. All this is, of course, consistent with our habits of using up youth in wars even when we do not let them vote. There are many implications to cutting out the years in which young people can be immature in the sense that they are free to grow and are not expected to be full-grown. We are plundering their birthright, making it more difficult for them to achieve their identity, and crippling them for the challenges of intimacy. Young people pay the price in their later-life relationships when adults do not assist them to work through the developmental challenges appropriate to the period of youth.

It is no wonder so many of youth's songs are sad ballads, tinged with longing for a gentle understanding of friendship and love. Overanxious and competitive adults, striving for vicarious life in their offspring, have taken away something that can never be given back to them, their youth. Beyond this, youth have been extensively manipulated and exploited to serve adult commercial and emotional ends. This adult generation has become noted for ravaging our natural resources, killing off streams, cutting down forests, and not giving either of them time to grow again. Far more serious is the despoiling of youth. The stripping of the years in which young people should establish the foundation they need to move forward in real love and trust.

Youth has hardly been given the opportunity to deal with the problems which are characteristically worked out in the preadult years, their understanding of their relationship toward sex and toward authority. Both of these are intimately connected with the meanings of mature love. It is not, of course, that the young do not speak and demonstrate about these notions; they are for the one and against the other in great numbers. What is clear is that they do not understand either one of them very profoundly and that the adult world has been unwilling to help them very much. Adults have not only failed to provide models of loving relationship, they have tried to squeeze the solutions to their own problems from the young. Youth has quite rightly identified the hypocrisy and inconsistency of its elders and has seen precious little that it can depend on in return. In fact, the young have been turned to by the adults who are desperate for models themselves. They have been bled dry by adults who have demanded from them a leadership which, despite their good instincts, they cannot be expected to provide. It is the failure of mature relationship in the adult world that has, on the one hand, cut short the real meaning of youth, and on the other, has burdened youth with responsibilities that it is not yet strong enough to bear.

There is, in fact, a new romanticism abroad in the land, a blend of sentimentalism and yearning that seems to touch the middle-aged most of all. For the members of the so-called "command generation," the harvesters of our affluence, show many signs of it. It manifests itself in those who seem desperate to find their youth again, whether it is in their cosmetic battle against aging, their slightly creaking efforts at being "swingers," or their seeming lack of a well-defined set of adult values. There is, however, a plaintive quality about some of the middle-aged in that so many appear to be searching still for the maturity which they should already possess.

Perhaps the chief manifestation of this phenomenon is the way so many adults lean on youth for direction and support these days. It may be to wipe away some feelings of guilt they have for seeming to have failed youth that leads many to endorse unquestioningly the yearnings of our youth culture. Perhaps, as sociologist Bennett Berger has observed, some moral critics have accepted the premise that "the young are simply better people than the old or middle-aged, and hence even a belief in juvenocracy." ("The New Stage of American Man-Almost Endless Adolescence," the New York *Times Magazine*, Nov. 2, 1969, p. 131.) In any case, many adults clearly seek identity from their children rather than share their own with them. Instead of offering affirmation to youth, many adults desire to receive it from them. In place of offering models for the young of what it means to be grown-up, some adults put their energies into imitating the young.

Some adults, for example, go to great lengths to seem "relevant" to the young. In order to achieve this posture, they try to move down into youth's activities, ideologies, and enthusiasms. They want to be like youth in order to be liked by youth. The difficulty here, of course, is that adults who wish truly to be relevant to youth can only do this by maintaining their adult status with some conviction and integrity. The task, a principal dynamic of human growth and development, has been and always will be the same. It is to bring youth into the adult world, to share one's life without yielding one's maturity. This is precisely what it means to offer a model with which youth will want to identify. The grownup need not be perfect, but he must have dealt adequately with his own problems of identity if he is to be an agent capable of helping the young to grow themselves. Obviously this demands that the adult be open and understanding toward the young, but he can do this without giving up his own maturity.

Indeed, if one tries to understand what the young mean when they speak of relevance, one senses that their search is very much for the enlarging and transcendent values which the Christian tradition should have preserved for them. They are looking for something to touch them deep inside; their language reflects this desire very clearly. They want to go beyond affluence even though they are very much attached to it. That is precisely one of the sources of their conflicts, one that will only be resolved with authentic adult help. They are looking for values to live by even though their extended adolescence may shield them from many of the more cruel aspects of life. There is a hunger in youth, a ravening desire for life itself. The young are, without too much exaggeration, really looking for those who can help them to understand the meaning of love. They are betrayed by the adults whose own difficulties with loving make them feast emotionally on the youth of today.

Probably the most striking example of this is the muddy, marijuana-filled Woodstock Music and Art Fair, which, in the essays and comments of many adults, has been translated into a vision of Eden. This happening, about which most of the great newspapers and news magazines wrote with the identity-seeking enthusiasm I have been discussing, attracted hundreds of thousands of young people for a weekend of peace and music in the summer of 1969. There was no great violence despite the crowds, and because of this, many adults, afflicted with the new romanticism, have been willing to overlook everything else that happened and to turn away from the deeper questions that the event must bring to mind. Perhaps the hills were pulsing with the aspirations of the young for peace and gentleness, but they also resonated with passivity, purposelessness, and a large degree of irresponsibility. It was youth searching rather than celebrating, youth looking for meaning rather than youth establishing a beachhead on the new century. One is not surprised by the widespread usage of drugs, the casual alfresco sex, and the unformed set of values proclaimed by many of the participants. The young thought the trip to Woodstock worthwhile because what they were unconsciously seeking, a better understanding of life, was worthwhile.

Indeed, the comments of many of the young who were involved tell us just how much a quest was represented by this affair. There is something touching in the accounts of the young who were deeply moved by the experience as one of closeness with other persons who seemed to care about each other and who seemed to be able to talk the same language. There was, in fact, an aura of the feeling that an adolescent experiences when his first exploration of friendship tinges all his days with a golden hue. There was also something terribly fragile about the relationships of that weekend. If we put aside the pot, the irresponsibility that left a littered countryside for somebody else to clean up, one senses that youth was looking for the meaning of human relationship. Even the rock anthems of their generation echoed this longing across the hills. One might understand the event best as a massive search for something that the young people have lost or that has been denied them by the circumstances of the modern world. They were looking for human contact, reaching out tentatively and without great self-assurance, making all the mistakes that the young are bound to make when adults have failed to give them the assistance and the example that they need.

Indeed, there is evidence to suggest just how readily many of the young would respond to adults who could give evidence of being able to speak to them intelligibly on questions of moral value. Some research, summarized recently by Kenneth Keniston, points to the moral sensibility of youth, a finely honed cutting edge of concern about right and wrong. This is intensified to some extent, according to Keniston, by the existence of a life stage called youth, from which the young can maintain a certain sustained separation from the world of adult moral problems. The existence of this sensibility and the possibility that it could be developed in larger numbers of the young is the kind of signal to which educators and Churchmen should readily respond. It indicates a clear meeting ground for the older and younger generations on one of the most traditional of turfs, moral concern.

The unrecognized and saddest part of this and similar affairs is the faulty and immature response of the adults who, with a great sigh of relief, were eager to see the festival as a great step forward for mankind. This, of course, is to compound youth's problem in several ways. First, it tells them that their judgment about their elders is accurate, that they have little to offer them of lasting value, and that they preserve certain traditions of education, culture, and religious behavior out of sheer hypocrisy. One recalls in this regard the painful words of a Harvard sophomore who felt deeply the drift of his own life and the loneliness of his own alienation:

If I had been brought up in Nazi Germany—supposing I wasn't Jewish—I think I would have had an absolute set of values, that is to say, Nazism, to believe in. In modern American society, particularly in the upper-middle class, a very liberal group, where I am given no religious background, where my parents always said to me, "if you want to go to Sunday School, you *can*," or "if you want to take music lessons, you *can*," but "it's up to *you*," where they never did force any arbitrary system of values on me—what I find is that with so much freedom, I am left with *no* value system, and in certain ways I wish I had a value system forced on me, so that I could have something to believe in. (Steven Kelman, "These Are Three of the Alienated," the New York *Times Magazine*, Oct. 22, 1967, p. 39)

There is a terrible pain in a statement like this, one that evidences the basic betrayal of youth by adults who fail at being truly generative because of their own confusion and the lack of depth in their own convictions about the true values of life. Many of these adults manifest their own emotional poverty in their great attachment to the favorable response of youth to them. They seem terrified at the prospect that even the slightest reflective word on their part might cause youth not to like them. This is the height of the new romanticism which has cloaked Woodstock in a golden haze and freed adults from the need to deal at greater depth with their own responsibilities for the next generation. These new romantics are trying to make something out of youth's searching that is just not there yet. As they do it, they place a considerable burden on the young, who are understandably confused when they are asked to provide a philosophy of life that will reassure their parents when, in reality, they are desperately in need of adults who can pass on something of lasting value to them. Adults who have not worked out their own values are basically disrespectful of youth, which has a right to something better from them.

In a sense, adults with convictions should make youth uneasy. A person who has learned something about love, the meaning of trust, and the nature of commitment to other persons, should prove challenging and unsettling for those who are drifting along on the tide of the supposed new life stage of youth. A remark made to a college-psychiatrist colleague of mine perfectly illustrates this. The young man was struck by the peace and self-confidence of his therapist. He found out that the psychiatrist was a committed religious person, somebody who believed in something and tried to live by it, somebody who did not back off in the face of his own self-proclaimed relativistic philosophy of life. He said to the psychiatrist one day, "You know, that you are sure of yourself and that you really believe in something, is very threatening to me." The psychiatrist was communicating an adult level of life with which everybody must come to terms sooner or later. There were relationships to be worked out, values to be integrated, decisions to be made, and a consistent pattern of life to be followed. The psychiatrist was a sign of all these things, a challenge to the growth of the college student. In some similar way, adults must present this kind of challenge to all youth, an unsettling challenge to grow that is supported by the presence of elders ready to help youth in the struggle.

When adults fail to represent the human values of love and friendship in action, they fail to help youth learn how to love in an active and positive manner. They reinforce the large-scale passivity which is already a serious problem for young people. Indeed, what has been proclaimed as a new life stage is for many a time of regression rather than advancement. It is a period when they ignore or retreat from situations which demand active and long-term commitment of themselves. Youth has become a time when the mobile young can move back and forth and sideways but not necessarily forward. It is no surprise to find many youths confused about the meaning of love. For some it means being loved, being cared for, and not being challenged to grow. This is a very primitive and undeveloped notion, of course, one that is complicated by parents whose own relationships have not seemed to ring true to their children.

Acceptance is a very important ingredient in love for the young. Indeed acceptance is a great value in any stage of human relationship. For the young, however, this is often acceptance which has no reference point and value, acceptance which cannot see people against the background of time, responsibility, or any sense of realizing fully their own potential. There is a streak of passivity in this acceptance, a wariness of challenging the other to produce, a willingness to accept any behavior, no matter how flawed or diminished, on the grounds of some vague personalism. Acceptance is not quite as protoplasmic as this. The young have hold of the edge of something important, but they clearly need the assistance of older people who can help them fully to develop an understanding of what it means to accept another person without abandoning a sense of reality or a set of values at the same time.

So, too, the young, despite their rhetoric of involvement, tend to move back in a way from engagement with other people when this is marked by any of the demands on the self that go along with having faith in or hoping for another person. They want closeness, but they are not sure they want to or can pay the price of friendship and love. The world looks too disillusioning to them to give themselves unreservedly to the future. At the bottom of this hesitancy to commit the self or to accept the hazards of loving that goes beyond the moment is a terrible fear that all of this could come to nothing.

Sociologist Jeffrey Hadden, in a recent study on the younger generation, describes this in another way. He writes of youth's:

retreat into privatism . . . there to resist further inroads into their personal domain. Their predominant mood, then, takes the form of rejection of authority and the de-

sire to follow their own modes of conduct. . . . I have
come to see the danger of a privatism ethic that turns into
a kind of romantic withdrawal. Like the drug trip into the
self, retreat into the totally personal world can be an escape from responsibility to others and to the society. . . .
The critical question is whether their social idealism,
though abstractly stated and daintily enforced in private
life, will be molded into a commitment to transform society toward their goals or will it become the hypocrisy of
the present generation raised to a higher level of rhetoric?
("A Private Generation," *Psychology Today*, Oct. 1969,
p. 68)

It is clear that youth does not know the way and that
adults pile the sins of their own generation on them when
they fail to place themselves into a relationship with youth
which will help them to grow and to understand the values
which will open them up to each other and to the world
around them in a truly loving way. There are great difficulties in loving. To a generation tempted to privatism,
adults must manifest a model of increased selflessness.
This is an extremely urgent and serious task that is not
solved by adults who hold their breath in hopes that everything will turn out all right in the end. It is more pressing
than the problem of the pollution of our physical environment. It involves the preservation of our human environment in which the young will still be able to discover and
enjoy friendship and love.

IT SHOWS UP IN SEX

"There may be some things better than sex," W. C. Fields is supposed to have said, "and some things may be worse, but there is nothing exactly like it." And there is nothing that holds a mirror up to man in exactly the way sex does. For in his sexual behavior, attitudes, and fantasies, man says a lot about himself. Probably the most significant thing man's management of his sexuality indicates is the degree of his over-all growth and development. It is true for man in general and for man in particular: Sexuality is expressive and reflective of how fully human he is.

Man has really only recently begun to listen carefully to the messages of his sexuality. He has, of course, always been fascinated by it, as the phallic shards of ancient monuments and the remnants of his first love poems tell us. But man has had to live through centuries made dark by ignorance and emotional inhibition. He did not cease to be sexual during these times. The indirect, hypocritical, or symbolic forms of sex that abounded during Victorian-like eras revealed the sharp edges and the deep shadows of the classic puritan profile. So, too, the present moment of heralded sexual liberation tells us something about the maturity of man on the verge of a new century. Man's sexuality and the complex of feelings he has about it reflect his attitudes toward himself and toward his neighbor. His sexual behavior tells us whether his reaching out to others is tender and respectful or clutching and selfish; it reveals whether man is growing or not in true friendship and love.

Sexuality fits into the human framework of love, completing it and setting it off from all other human experiences. Healthy sexuality doesn't come out of diet foods, fun-in-the-sun nudity, or exciting new patent medicines. It flourishes when two people love one another and keep working at developing their relationship with one another despite the pile-up of life's problems. Sexuality is full of sunrise when lovers have been able to work their way through the darkness of misunderstandings and new learning that are so much a part of their lives. Sexuality that arises from a growing relationship keeps on growing itself. That is why it is such a revealing sign of man as he is found in the human condition, man always in process, man trying to move forward in growth.

One is moved rather than outraged by the abundant evidence of human immaturity that is reflected in the so-called sexual freedom of our day. So much of what passes for sophistication and enlightenment tells how far man has to go rather than how far he has come. The temptation, especially for Churchmen, is always to denounce erotica and other symbols of immature sexuality. This can be done in a rising tone of voice and with a pinch of righteous indignation, a combination that men of the cloth don't get to use much any more. Here, after all, is a chance to put sex back into the spotlight of sin. So a famous American bishop, asked to comment on priests who got married, chose to speak of sheep and pigs who fall into the mud. The sheep get up, but the pigs stay in to wallow in the ooze. This shows how easily the black and white rhetoric of denunciation can be pressed back into service when something connected with sexuality comes up. It is far harder to try to catch and understand the deeper meaning of the sexual behavior which we see in our day. This is difficult, not only because old attitudes lie close to the most renewed-looking surface, but also because most of us are still too embarrassed and uneasy to talk realistically about sex. We tend to speak defensively, too loudly or too softly, and this makes it hard for us to be truly understanding. It makes it hard for us to hear the language of sexuality either in ourselves or in others.

We really need a more compassionate feeling for man. He has had quite a struggle up through the centuries, trying to understand himself and the world he dominates. Right now he is telling us about himself and his need for sounder human relationships, for the simple healing of friendship and love, even as he acts out his contemporary sexual hangups. Beneath all of it is man in process, at one point bizarre and distorted, at another wounded and defensive, and at yet others showing some effort to get himself humanly together so that he can live harmoniously with his sexuality. The positive side of an era of sexual liberation reveals man approaching his sexuality again, overcompensating for but not completely overcoming years of being cowed by guilt and fear with a bravado that has a strong adolescent flavor to it. The negative side reveals, in the range of problems connected with his sexuality (most of which have shown up before in history), just how much growth he has yet to achieve. It is my contention that these difficulties reflect the frustrations of man when he has broken sex off from love in human relationships. I further believe that the Church, while it has denounced man's sexual problems consistently over the centuries, has actually been a major force in contributing to them.

Even a brief review of man's present difficulties with sexuality support this case. Perhaps it is more significant than we suppose that man now speaks far more openly about sex than he did at times in the past. Formerly, he tolerated more pretense, a Victorian veneer that was bolstered by repressive defenses. His sexuality was there all the while, knotted into just as many hangups as man knows today. Then, however, it was not talked about so publicly, hardly admitted into consciousness even though its dynamics flourished in the kind of underworld or double life that man adopts when he is hypocritical. Sigmund Freud lived and worked in such a cultural atmosphere. He did not invent sexual dynamics; he found them strongly operative in the patients with whom he worked, and he spent his life trying to understand it all. Man was clearly not integrated in that era. His sexuality was compartmentalized, locked away behind tight defenses, a West Berlin lying in the midst of alien territory, full of tempting light and pleasure, but a dangerous round trip for the average person.

Today's preoccupation with sexuality, while a sign of immaturity, is at least a step forward from the world where it could not be mentioned even though it had a vigorous subterranean life. Howsoever ill-framed and confused are today's questions and answers, they at least show man shedding his hypocrisy, and attempting to understand his sexuality as a rich and rightful part of himself. He has, in other words, dropped the awful defensive system that allowed him to lead a divided life, reassuring himself of his propriety on the one hand while he guiltily enjoyed an isolated sexuality on the other. He is still having enormous difficulty in integrating his sexuality, but man is more open and less ready to be deceitful about it.

I think we can hear modern man saying, for example, "I am trying to get free of fear." Much of his present sexual expression indicates that he is attempting to shed the anxiety, multiplied in Victorian darkness, whose weight has been such a terrible burden for him. He is powerfully, if somewhat blindly, motivated to dispel the suspicion and uneasiness that have settled like smoky clouds around his sexuality. Man is moving at trying to be more human, trying to grow, and yet still lost, straining to find the direction in which he should move. Man, if you will, is trying to get to know himself.

The common denominator for the present symbolic sexual expression of man is found in man's estrangement from friendship and love. When he is confused about the meaning of these, it shows up clearly in his sexuality. The dropping of repressive defenses just makes it easier for us to see this. For example, the present passion for the quick uninvolved and uninvolving sexual episode documents man's inability to take on the responsibility of relationship with another. A recent French survey revealed that men were showing a new preference for the isolated and emotionally uninvolving experience of sex, variety rather than richness being the key element. The tradition of the mistress is being eroded by this trend, precisely because it demands some kind of consistency and continuity in responsible relationship. Much better, then, the experience without antecedental or consequent emotional claims. The quick "score," our language catching the cold mathematics of it, can only be preferred by men who do not want to be bothered by the challenge of love. They clearly separate sex from relationship in this kind of experience, isolating themselves as the friendless generation which searches for but does not find fulfillment. This kind of person points, in his sexual behavior, to the real problem of undeveloped human relationships that lies beneath it.

The person who thus separates sex from the meaning he only has when his total self is engaged with others never deals with the challenges that are the vitalizing aspects of love. He need not learn the meaning of faithfulness, for example, because there is no one to whom he commits himself. He need not hope, because, just as episodic sex has no past, neither has it any future. He does

not love because he has insulated himself from the flow
of life with others, which is its only setting. Man hung
up on self-saving and self-defeating sex as isolated pleasure
stifles the impulse to relate to others because love dangerously demands that he continue to grow. All the potential
meaning of human relationships, the whole direction in
which man must go if he is to fulfill himself, is brought
into focus by his restlessness and lack of deep satisfaction
with this kind of behavior.

It is the same in other aspects of present-day sexuality.
When man strives for a species of freshness and spontaneity in sexual relationships, for a renewed understanding of
playfulness, he is obviously moving in the direction of
growth. But this growth is not easy, and it is especially
difficult when man is trying to find his way pretty much on
his own. He can slip backward as well as step forward.
He can get stuck and settle, as many moderns have, for
the thrills of an undeveloped level of personality. The
sado-masochism of the day, decked out in the deceptively
modernistic robes of the *avant-garde*, is still behavior that
bubbles up from the preadolescent wells of personality.
Variously described as sophisticated or decadent, the
"kinky" sex of the contemporary world actually points to
the severe growth problem of modern man.

The so-called fruits of sexual liberation are bitter if they
amount to little more than a self-centered plunge back
into the world of primitive sexual energy. There is no
doubt that every man feels the erotic edges of the earliest
layers of his personality many times during his life. There
is something deep and strong about taking and being
taken, about looking and being looked at, and other
primordial experiences that a man never forgets. They are
close to the bedrock of his personality, powerful currents
whose energies are meant to be assimilated into the fully
grown personality. Traces of these forces endure, as in-

deed they must, even after man achieves mature sexuality. They contribute to the intensity and the significance of adult sexuality, in which echoes from all the levels of man's development are heard again. These experiences, however, represent the foundations for later personality growth rather than the term of it. The fact that we are presently witnessing a great deal of undeveloped sexuality points again to the personal growth problem of modern man. Far better that the influence and authority of education and religion be felt in assisting man to integrate these impulses in more mature stages of personal development than that they merely indict or criticize him for being immature. Immature themselves are those who capitalize on these undeveloped aspects of man by trying to sell him on the idea that they represent real liberation and maturity.

An overlapping area of our culture finds a new celebration of the human body on stage, screen, and in newer forms of the encounter-group styles of therapy. Outlandish and immature as this often is, it is at least a move away from regarding the body as a prison for the spirit. It is also a sign of man's efforts, barely conscious to himself, of trying to re-establish the unity of human personality. Man is, in other words, blundering toward a mature value through a whole range of immature behaviors. The point is that the steps to maturity are necessarily immature. The problem arises, as it does in the present, when man settles for or gets stuck at some mid-point in the ladder of development, and when no one really helps him with understanding or assistance to complete his journey. Sadly enough, much of the nudity in entertainment reflects the somewhat fragile and two-sided effort man makes to be at home in his own body. Much of it is developmentally narcissistic and homosexual, a celebration, in drama critic Walter Kerr's phrase, of impotence rather than of the mature power appropriate to sharing and giving life. It is an effort to feel whole again, an attempt to rediscover the profound significance of touching and being touched, of that subtle communication that necessarily involves man's body. The full realization of the meaning of the psychosomatic unity of the person is attained only in the far reaches of authentic friendship and love. There man and his body are more comfortably one, and his integrated sexuality is truly expressive of his unity.

Closely akin to these developments is the apparent increase of sexual apathy in many males. Psychiatrist Ralph Greenson describes sexual apathy as "behavior which indicates a conscious indifference, disinterest, and coldness toward sexual intercourse." While little research has been done on this subject, such apathy is a clinical symptom of the troubles that are dogging man during the era of sexual liberation. Man finds himself not quite up to it, worn out or frightened off by the escalation of the demands for his sexual performance. Unreasonable and uneven demands are only made, of course, when there is real lack of understanding of human sexuality. This cannot help but be the case when sexuality is stripped away from the only setting in which it can grow, the living personality of man.

Greenson sees this developing apathy as man's response to the increasing sexual assertiveness of women as well as to other cultural factors that affect man's picture of himself. He finds in his clinical experience, for example, a mounting hostility toward women on the part of men who are threatened by the new-style feminine independence and aggression. Others see this apathy as the inevitable result of sex broken off from human relationship, a telling expression of impotence in isolation from true friendship and love. What is interesting is that, whatever the dynamics of the shift in the relationship of men and women in our culture, the signs show up in sexual behavior. Sexual behavior is a profound part of the secret language which man speaks all the time, and by means of which he reveals the pressures of relationships which he does not feel competent to handle.

When man hurts in some way that he will not face or cannot put directly into words he plays a dumb show of his inner pain to himself and to the world. This expresses his problem symbolically. Those who would help man must decode these symbols and strive to assist him to overcome the obstacles and conflicts which hinder his growth. The Church has not only lost touch with man who struggles this way; it has contributed to the isolation of sexuality from love and the meaning of human relationships. It has been, as a human institution grown creaky, insensitive to man's symbolic sexuality. This is a betrayal of its own healthy Gospel traditions, which are lighted up by a great wisdom and appreciation of human sexuality. The Church's involvement in this problem is coming to light because it is being challenged to come closer to man, to enter more deeply into his life, to be friend rather than a master to man. In this challenge to relate more closely to man, the Church's failure to integrate its sexuality has become more obvious. Indeed, in no area has it spoken more confusedly in recent years than in terms of man's sexuality. It has revealed an outdated vocabulary as well as a divided and suspicious model of man. The Institutional Church's failure to keep up with man has shown up in sexuality.

The difficulty is that the Church is only beginning to shake loose from the paralysis of the centuries. In fact, the struggles of the Church to come alive again show up in sex too. The discussions of birth control and celibacy are first cousins to the other sexual symbolism of our time. They are signs of men trying to understand their sexuality and of attempting to reintegrate it into a fully developed picture of themselves. These discussions indicate man's search for the dimensions of life that give support and meaning to human sexuality. These are, of course, friendship and love, the only elements that enable man to put himself fully together. These are, needless to say, deep Gospel values as well, but values that, for one reason or another, became like a foreign language on the tongues of many Churchmen.

I think that the Church is attempting to recover its lost view of man but that it will have increased difficulty in doing this until it can admit just how much it contributed to the separation of sex from love. The Church did this, however, with great thoroughness and with tremendous force. Sex, as has been commented on often enough, was seen not as a healthy part of growing man but as something marred, something less than good, something tolerated for preserving the race. So, too, the Church kept people at a distance from one another, making them uneasy about their own bodies and their sexual powers, accentuating their estrangement from what was fully human in the process. Somewhere along the line, the very idea of the deep and healthy meaning of bodily contact was sicklied over with the pale cast of suspicion. The wonder that lovers should know of the confirming and nourishing power of their bodily communication was checked by a generation of Churchmen who elevated *noli me tangere* to the level of a counsel if not a commandment. Other examples, already mentioned by numerous other observers, such as the overevaluation of virginity, and the great suspicion of friendship and intimacy, are significant because they contributed so powerfully to the isolation of sex from the human experience of love. Without giving further examples, it is enough to note the widespread and controlling effect of this non-integrated view of the human person. It was multiplied, after all, in pronouncements from pulpits, the application of canon law, and the pervasive effects of a widespread educational system. Now the Church is not the chief or only villain, to be sure. But, as the instrumentality charged to preserve a thorough understanding of man, it grew distracted or sleepy and failed to sense just what a distorted and unhealthy image of man and his sexuality it absorbed in the course of time. The Church came not to be the champion of spontaneous and loving relationships, but the guardian of careful and controlled ones; it became not the preserver and integrator of man's basic relationships to himself and his neighbor, but an agency that divided and estranged man from friendship and love.

Now a new generation, anxious to purify the Christian message and to put man back into proper perspective, suffers precisely because of the Church's strangely acquired but strongly developed uneasiness toward man and his sexuality. This generation wants to integrate sexuality, but it is painfully discovering just how big a job this is when sexuality has been compartmentalized for years. There is little wonder that longings come out in embarrassingly immature ways at times. The renewing Church is full of symbols, from the mini-skirted and seductive nun supposedly protesting Dow Chemical but really acting out something quite different on a well-known Catholic campus, to the tug of war that has made whether priests are married or not the most disproportionately talked-about question of the day, that tell us the struggle to integrate sexuality is under way and somewhat irreversible. The Church has, in any case, contributed a good deal, and quite unconsciously, to the problem. It remains for it to come fully to terms with it so that it can help all men rediscover the meaning of friendship and love.

This is the task of all the Churches, the proclamation of the Gospel that unites man in the love that is the life of God. A chief task for any Church is the creation of the environment of community that has its roots in the Gospel vision of man whose destiny is to achieve the highest level of human development in the integrating experience of love. Man's yearning for this is expressed in his struggling efforts to integrate all the aspects of himself, including his sexuality.

The message has many levels and a mixture of meanings: man yearning for the light that evaporates fear and for the freedom to be himself; man confused and cowed by the pain of relationships unreached or gone sour; man tangled in the shredded but enticing web of primitive sexual experiences; man hung up on reaching other persons in a trusting and loving way. Human sexual behavior, like litmus paper in a chemical reaction, sensitively reflects man in process, man trying to muster up his real identity from a tragically disordered set of experiences.

What shows up in sex in our era does not express a new maturity as much as it does man's shuffling and sometimes sideways movements in his struggle to grow. Man is, in some over-all sense, growing in a gangling and uncoordinated way, somewhat the way all adolescents do. His intelligence is extraordinary, and his muscles ripple across the earth he has tamed. Emotional growth has not, however, kept pace, and so man suffers the same kinds of problems all adolescents do. He looks grown-up, but he is unsure of himself inside; he is fascinated by the throbbing strength of his sexual powers, but he is also afraid and uneasy about them; he wants to touch others in the mysterious relationships of friendships and love, but he is shy and awkward; he is made to be a man, but in an instant, he can revert to less developed forms of relationship, destroying tenderness with aggression, alienating himself from what he wants and needs most, open and trusting relationships.

Organized religion has a quite specific challenge to respond to man with compassionate understanding of his problems of growth and his need for the life-giving experiences of friendship and love. Indeed, authentic religion will flower when it has joined itself fully to the task of reintegrating its image of man and is able once again to nourish and celebrate his full humanity. Friendship and love are at the heart of genuine religion, and these are the values that inform a healthy society and a world in which man can really become more of himself. It is not in the nature of things to expect man to find a back door to an Eden where he will play innocently again in the shadow of the Lord God. There will be no Utopia where, unscarred by any guilt at all, man will find uninterrupted delight in the pleasures of his unblemished flesh. Those are the dreams of the sexual liberators and the pharmaceutical prophets, dreams that will always beckon man but will never come true.

Authentic sexual freedom comes about only in the lives of those who can see sexuality as a vital aspect of their relationship with other persons. These people do not look at sex as the end of all loneliness or the automatic open sesame of human relationship. They know that friendship and love precede and irradiate sexuality as a deeply appropriate and expressive aspect of man. But this knowledge does not come easy, or all at once; it only gets deeper as it unfolds across the years. Friendship and love are a fabric made strong by the strands of suffering and patience, understanding and sensitivity, living and dying, that are in its weave. People who have begun to learn the lessons of friendship and love can at last see sexuality in its place, which is considerably less than the whole horizon of life.

Indeed, until we take trust and human sharing more seriously, our ears will be filled with the language of sexual liberation, but our hearts will feel painfully empty of the love that really makes us free.

LOVE IS PATIENT

The world is full of definitions of love; wise men have tried to get it into words for centuries. But for all the generations of poems and statues, and now balloons and banners, love remains without the last word said about it. It is, above all else, elusive and mysterious. Love is many things but it is not the sum of them; it is easy to recognize and experience but painfully difficult to describe with satisfaction. Love does not easily fit into categories nor is it found only at certain times or in certain relationships. Wherever and whenever it is found, however, authentic love has certain watermarks that are always there.

That is what St. Paul was trying to tell his Christian community at Corinth in his famous exposition on love. I have often wondered why he wrote about love to his Corinthian converts at that particular time. In an immediately preceding section he discusses the Christians' unity even though they have differing gifts which they are called to use for the sake of each other. He seems to have detected a certain spiritual competition in his flock, a certain flowering of religious ambition which endangered the balance of the Christian community. Paul seems to be saying, "You Corinthians, despite your gifts, will have it all wrong unless you get down to business about the nature of love." We are all different, he tells them, and it is in the climate of our differences from one another that love becomes important. So he writes, "Be ambitious for the higher gifts," and then he quickly adds, "and I am going to show you a way that is better than any other." Nothing he or anybody else does will mean much if it is not motivated

by love; just gongs booming and cymbals clashing. He
goes on to describe love in a way that has never really
been improved upon. He says, first of all, that love is
patient.

This concept does not appeal very much to either young
or old in a world where man's appetite for speed records,
whether in running the mile or flying across the ocean, is
never really satisfied. It is all the more difficult in an age
where the delay of any gratification is looked on as an evil
or at least an unfortunate impediment to the good life.
Tremendous cultural forces urge man on to get what he
wants now and to postpone the consequences until later.
This is true in getting into debt in order to get the luxuries
of life; it is also true in the level of human relationships
where intimacy must be instant and where, for example,
sexual experience is no longer regarded as a goal but rather
as a beginning of relationship.

It is hard for people who have been conditioned by the
values of immediate gratification to pause for a moment
and ponder the meaning of love as something patient.
That means, after all, that love can wait, that love can
suffer, that love is not in a hurry, and that an appreciation
of this is indispensable to any kind of authentic and mature loving. Wise men and women know that patience and
suffering are essential characteristics of love even as they
are of life itself. Patience, after all, is not procrastination
or hesitation. It is not putting off some action of life out
of fear; it is rather a whole way of presenting oneself in
relationship to others that indicates a sense of respect for
the other and an understanding of the way all things, including love, grow.

You can think about love as something patient in many
different ways and still not exhaust its meaning. Friends
and lovers must be patient with one another, not crossing
the borders of each other's private lives prematurely, not

trampling on the inner space of the other heedlessly or selfishly. This kind of patience only means something to the person who can look at the other as distinct from himself, with a separate life, separate needs, and a right to have these respected. Even those who love each other most intensely come up against the mystery of their distinctness from one another and of the ultimate impenetrability of some core of each other's personality. They cannot tear away or obliterate what makes them separate individuals. Indeed, it is of the essence of creative love that separate persons, with distinct characteristics, assert themselves in relationship to one another. This kind of sharing brings people very closely together, but it never obliterates the boundaries of their personalities. Indeed, one of the pains known to all real lovers is the impossibility of merging themselves into one identity.

The frustration that lovers face because they cannot, even through the most intimate sexual sharing, become forever one can only be tolerated by those who have learned the meaning of patience. In their patience they do not respond to this frustration with the angriness or the hostility of one whose path has been blocked by some obstacle. They sense rather that their separate personalities, even with the unknown depths which yield only slowly to each other, are essential to the nature of their love. This is a hard kind of learning, one that demands special sensitivity and the readiness to take a long-range view of life. Lovers must be patient if they are to grow in love and understanding.

Patience means a readiness to suffer. There is no suffering more exquisite than that which is known by those who love one another. One of the simplest truths of all time tells us that lovers can hurt each other precisely because they mean so much to each other. They learn, over the years, each other's weak spots; in a strange way, they know just how to move in on each other with maximum effect. Only a great deal of patience can help two people to stay in relationship to one another after they have learned so much about each other's weaknesses and how to get quickly at the jugular of each other's emotions. That is a part, that dangerous knowledge of the fabric of love, but it is only a part of it. When patience dies, this special understanding of where and how to hurt looms larger in the relationship until it has destroyed it altogether. Only patient love keeps people who know each other's faults and failings, and how to capitalize on them, together. This is not an easy thing by any means.

But love suffers in other ways as well. There is surely nothing that is more at the core of any love relationship than the realization of how lovers really die to themselves if they are to give life to one another. This is clearly one of the strong aspects of the patient quality of love. It lights up the little things as well as big ones and sets the pattern for the life in which yielding up the self for the sake of the other never really does come to an end. It just takes on new forms of expression. It is the counterpoint in every person's life of the very mystery of redemption itself, the living out of the mystery of life in Christ that is real religion. People who love each other have the difficult task of trying to share as intimately as possible even when they know that their separateness can never be fully erased. Neither man nor woman can have things fully his or her way any more, from running the house to raising the children to making love to each other. Life is something they experience together, and it demands the surrender of the self in a sensitivity to each other that they cannot allow to grow dull merely because of the burden of the years and the boredom of routine. Lovers who remain alive to each other have learned to die to themselves for the sake of their mutual love. This theme is essential to any grasp of the meaning of love at all.

There is no wonder that Paul put patience first in his way of describing love's characteristics. Patience is first because it is the strength that lovers need if their relationship is to retain its vitality. This is the kind of virtue that gets beneath the surface of a man or a woman to reveal his true identity. Those without an identity cannot possibly enter into the hazards of love because they have no storehouse of patience, no wisdom of life about its necessity. They simply cannot be patiently present to one another in any kind of relationship. Patience, in other words, is a source of strength and a sign of challenge that can only be understood by those who have reached a reasonable level of maturity. It does not have much meaning at all for people who are hollow and undeveloped.

Patience, then, is an active feature of love. It is not the exasperated putting up with one another, the mildly hostile enduring of one another's strange habits. It goes far deeper than that. It helps lovers to seek out an understanding of each other, facing their response according to whatever finer sensitivity to each other's needs. Patience is an active aspect of the mutual respect that lovers truly must have for one another. It is what sustains them through the strains and trials that are inevitable in any life; it is one of the supports for the bridge love makes across all the days of ordinary and undramatic lives.

Patience, one might say, is a neglected if not unheard of word to use in describing love in our day and age. All the arguments go quite counter to this. The young, we are told, do not discuss the nature of patience and sensitivity to one another's growth; they ponder rather whether to have premarital sexual relationships or not. The question of premarital sex relations is so often separated from the context of an ongoing relationship that it is remotely related to the dimensions of real love. Premarital sex short-circuits relationships often enough, blotting out everything else that goes into the process by which persons get to know each other. It is very effective, as has been noted earlier, in protecting people from the emotional consequences of relationship. As Rollo May has noted, "The Victorian person sought to have love without falling into sex; the modern person seeks to have sex without falling into love." (*Love and Will*, New York, W. W. Norton, 1969.) Premarital sex prevents people from learning what they should know in order to spend their lives together. To say that love must be patient would invite scorn from the so-called sophisticates of our day. This is, however, a superficial scorn that comes from persons who have not taken a very deep look at the full meaning of love.

People who have never learned to postpone gratification have a great deal of difficulty in learning the lessons of love. If you have always been able to have what you wanted at the moment you wanted it, then it is very hard to understand anything in life that does not come quickly and easily. There is a temptation to give up on it, to put it aside, and to settle for what can be gotten without delay. Pleasure, of course, can be achieved without delay, but this is by no means the same thing as lasting happiness. Pleasure can be derived in human relationships, especially at the level of sexuality, but all too often in an empty way that is far from being very human as well.

People unschooled in patience get caught at a level of development in which they cannot understand very well anything beyond pleasure, while at the same time they are not at all satisfied by the pleasures they do achieve. It is difficult for them to keep at anything that demands constant application, consistency of effort, and some deferral of reward. People like this are ready to hear the arguments for premarital sex and to accept the rationalizations which

justify it. At the same time, they may lose the possibility
of ever understanding something about the nature of love,
which alone can be a source of long-range satisfaction and
happiness for them. They are tricked by a glib and reassuring standard of values that tells them to take what they
can get when they can get it. A man or woman who accepts
this philosophy will find it difficult even to learn the beginnings of the kind of patience they will need to sustain
them in any relationship with another person. The concept
of sacrifice or dying to the self in view of the good of the
other will seem like something from a remote and irrele-
vant time. They will come up against the frustrations of
their relationship unequipped with the attitude and the
understanding of love's demands that will help them to
make a go of it. These people want intimacy and seek it
endlessly, even in a series of marriages, their quest and
their repeated failures dictated by their lack of understanding of the patience and waiting that goes into all love.

There is something almost infinitely sad about the people who do not understand the meaning of patience. They
cannot wait for anything, and so the mysterious meanings
of waiting and expectation are sealed off from them. Life
makes them wait often enough, and whether they like it
or not. But they meet delay with deep resentment, or
perhaps with the new style of apathy, that characterizes
their way of handling frustration. Patience, an active and
willing embrace of the situation, is vital in so many aspects
of loving. We must wait sometimes for love to grow, or
for each other to grow until we are strong enough to mean
it when we say, "I love you." We need patience as all the
funny shortcomings we all possess are absurdly and sharply
revealed. They are part of what we love when we accept
each other, even though we may spend a patient lifetime
trying to reform one another. Patience adds immeasurably
to the meaning of sexuality, both as a condition for the

development of the relationship and in the immediate
setting of sexual sharing. There must be patience for lovers
who cannot, for whatever reason, possess each other physi-
cally; this is the patience that sustains faithfulness when
those who love are separated. And patience is a measure
of the faith of those who love but who give their love for
the sake of the Gospel.

Those who have embraced the discipline of patience
know a very great fullness of love. The world turns around
for lovers who are reunited; a great fresh breeze blows
across the lives of men and women who have learned to
wait for one another. In their patience they have learned
part of the secret of being open to the Spirit who is the
breath of their life and their love. Lovers who have learned
to wait have had to deal with the daily, sometimes hourly,
business of dying to themselves. It was to patient lovers
that Christ said, "Your endurance will win you your lives."
(Luke 21:19.)

If a person is not willing to learn the lessons of patience,
he can only respond to his own inner impulses and will
find it difficult to allow others to grow at their own pace
or to find their own goals separate from those he sets for
them. The impatient person becomes possessive in a way
that poisons his relationships even as it sentences himself
to frustration and a progressive isolation. If a person is
serious about love, whether he is married or not, he has
to learn the meaning of patience. There are different reasons for this, although the dynamics are the same wherever
true love is involved.

Some married people must learn to live with many of
their desires interrupted by illness, unexpected separations, or the demands of a houseful of children. Their
lives, they learn quickly, are not really their own once they
have given themselves over to love. Without patience, they
will not have time to let their children grow or to let their

own love for each other grow even as it faces the obstacles
and difficulties that stand in its way. Sometimes a person
must put off marrying because of some other obligation,
perhaps to an aged or sick parent. There is a great deal of
pain and frustration in the sacrifice required when a person
delays the normal development of his own life out of a
sense of responsibility to others. So, too, a priest or religious may love and be loved deeply and yet, out of faith
that this love is given for him to share rather than to take
just for himself, try to live for the service of the whole
community of the Church. Patience is required in any and
all of these settings, a patience that knows the meaning of
delay and that is ready to face the challenge of death itself.
It is not unlikely that many of the Corinthians to whom
St. Paul wrote were just beginning to understand the
meaning and demands of love. It is not at all surprising
that he began by talking to them about patience.

✓ Respect for other

✓ Dying To self

✓ Respect for growth

IT IS NEVER JEALOUS

Of all the tremors that run through a man in a lifetime, none is more violent or destructive than jealousy. This is a powerful feeling, a special kind of anxiety, the trip switch of the worst of all anti-personal devices, human rage. Jealousy differs from envy, another feeling from the dark side of man, in that it is always hostile, arching its back and bristling in the presence of a rival. We can envy someone else's possessions without having strong feelings toward the person. But we are never jealous without wanting to hurt the other.

Jealousy, whether it is found in the child shunted off center stage by a new baby brother or in a triangle of uneasy lovers, is part of our vocabulary of insecurity. Jealousy, "the jaundice," as Dryden put it, "of the soul," comes to life when we are afraid of losing some affection to a rival. The welling feeling of jealousy is both expressive and instructive. It crumbles the fragile dams that ordinarily hold back our hostility. It catches us where it hurts, the strength of our jealousy revealing something about our maturity and the relative sureness of our friendships and love. When we are unsure of ourselves and our relationships to others we are vulnerable to the animal rages of jealousy. Nothing is more threatening to us than the loss of the love which we feel in some special way to be our own.

Jealousy provides an index of the depth of our relationships, a measure of our own integration and our capacity for trusting others and sharing ourselves with them. People who have not achieved a fairly well developed sense of their own identity find themselves taking more than they give in their close relationships. This kind of person, so common today, is prone to react jealously because the security of his relationships is so easily threatened. The amount of jealousy in a person's life is in inverse relationship to how well he knows and can be himself. Jealousy is a special hazard in the lives of those who are just learning how to love. No substance is as volatile as first love. Nor is it uncommon, for example, for individuals to experience the ravages of jealousy during their first wondrous but trying experiences of friendship. Friendship opens a new world to persons, lighting up treasures that they never knew existed; it is small wonder that they want to hold on to this new-found wealth and to protect it from anyone who might take it away from them. Jealousy is a polluted area in the otherwise fresh spring world in which persons learn to be friends with one another. It goes along with the fear of loss that stirs in our souls when we begin to share life emotionally with another.

Jealousy rides like an aura on the relationships we call first love. Through these relationships we may well be loving ourselves far more than the presumed beloved. This somewhat melancholy fact should be accepted as a stage in our growth, the inevitable possibility when we take our first tentative steps out of our own world in response to the influence of another person. Because we so often love ourselves at this stage, even though we are trying to reach out to another, we are constantly, if somewhat secretly, afraid of losing that which we love. The surges of jealousy, the anguish at seeing a friend become friendlier with someone other than ourselves, the pain when someone we prize disappoints us, the awkward ache of wanting some exclusive right to all the hours of the life of another: These are not at all unusual feelings for people just moving into friendship. The phenomenon is so intense and preoccupying, however, that it is a wonder that anybody ever survives it at all. Because there is no fail-safe mechanism in friendship, the uncertainties and inconsistencies that characterize its pursuit may give rise to a pervasive and dominating jealousy that leads an individual to do strange things to preserve the affection that he now needs more than anything else.

A terrible pain marks this period of life. It is necessary, as pain usually is, but sometimes the memory of it makes a man shy of friendship for the rest of his life. He may for many years be unduly on guard against other persons, withholding himself or doling himself out only under very precise conditions, a man very carefully protecting himself from the emotionally shredding things that can happen to you when you try to love. The first steps of friendship may be as harrowing as they are delightful. One thing is sure: Each individual must take them for himself. A man must learn firsthand and for himself about the things that are indispensable for later love and friendship. The fits of jealousy, the urges to possessiveness, the sweet sadness of so much of adolescent relationship: These are necessary hazards for the person who is still working out his own identity. They are the signs of a person in passage, the marks of the psychological rite of moving from childhood toward the estate of man, the evidence of the search for the inner confirmation that comes when we face the risks of human relationship.

Jealousy is understandable, even though blindingly painful, during that period of life when we are trying to put ourselves together in a psychologically unified manner. It lessens in strength as we move forward in understanding both ourselves and the meaning of our relationships with others. Jealousy is a tide that ebbs as we enter more deeply into our own selves and can realize how truly self-centered much of our first adventures in friendship really are. It is difficult to break away from the pool where our own reflection shines so brightly for us. Jealousy does, however, decline as we become more sure of the persons we really are, and thereby more capable of accepting our faulted selves and of opening ourselves to others for their own sake. There are many ways of describing the stages of friendship and love, moving from the narcissistic beginnings to highly developed mature love. For our purposes, we should note that the experience of jealousy falls off like a declining business graph as we move through these stages of growth. For those who are interested in knowing whether they are learning to love other people more truly, a simple but revealing question asks, "Am I less jealous than I used to be?" The answer to this tells us whether we have taken greater possession of ourselves and have established firmer relationships with others, relationships whose solidity makes us less subject to the fear that they might easily be lost.

When jealousy does not recede as a person grows older, it is a warning flare lighting up the inner insecurities which have never been resolved. Sometimes these are the residue of the broken relationships in which a person grew up in childhood. There are few things that make a man more possessive, more anxious to stake out the territorial domain of his adult relationships more precisely, than having lived in an emotional world that cracked and fell apart in his earliest years. It is hard to make up for the psychological scars people accumulate when they have suffered the emotional pains of a disintegrating parental relationship. The very quality needed to establish the kind of permanent relationship they most desire is trust. But trust for a person who has found those closest to him untrustworthy, is a very difficult thing to develop and give to others. The person estranged from trust is always under threat. What he prizes most could always be taken away, even as it happened to him while growing up. It is not strange that these people keep on their guard, lowering it only slowly in the presence of love from another that is truly redemptive. When a person does not have a later relationship in which he can grow to understand and exercise the kind of trust that extinguishes jealousy, he leads an extraordinarily painful life in which his emotional sensitivity opens a gap between him and other people which it is difficult for him ever to close.

The man or woman hurt seriously in friendship or love is wary of the next experience of it. When a person has been betrayed by someone to whom he has given trust, it is not easy to quiet the fears that the same thing could happen again. This person wants to make his love secure, bolting and fastening it against all who would take it away from him, reacting to others with great hostility and suspicion. These are the kind of people who sometimes perform violent actions, not excluding murder, when their jealousy is aroused. These people make the headlines regularly, the jealous husband or the jealous wife who has finally struck out at the person who is the source of threat to him. More often the hurting is a slower form of murder, an unending round of petty insurgency and counterinsurgency. This hostility is self-defeating. It does not bring greater security, only greater tension and pain. In the long run it destroys the world of relationship altogether.

One of the strongest but least identified forms of jealousy may be observed in persons who otherwise consider themselves quite religious. Psychologists who have studied religious behavior have tried to separate the characteristics of mature and immature religion. One of the signs of the latter, I submit, is the presence of a pious-faced jealousy that cannot bear the thought that love may be abroad in the land. For those people who are jealous in this manner (and hardly ever suspect it) cannot allow people to live their own lives separate from them and their control.

They are the religious figures who lend support to the caricature of the clergyman as a dour-faced person who cannot abide happiness in the lives of others. Nothing, I suppose, has harmed organized religion more than this subtle jealousy of the person so afraid to live a little himself that he must devote his life to a crusade against joy.

Jealousy is regularly found in a garden-variety form. This is not the product of a broken childhood, a betrayed romance, or some other major life disappointment. This jealousy is just the edge of the human condition showing. The uneasiness of this jealousy is found in the lives of ordinary people who are trying to learn to love each other. Most people recognize jealousy in themselves when they experience it. As long as they call it by the right name they can handle it in a reasonably mature manner. They can inspect their own emotional lives, sorting out fact from suspicion, sifting out the reasons for the experience of jealousy, and bringing them into the light of day when this is necessary. While this is not the simplest of processes, it is the ordinary way in which people work through their own emotional experience. Frequently, just the frank admission of their own jealousy (or fear or anger or whatever) is enough to break its strength and bring the person back into full control of himself. Nobody, after all, has devised a serum against the feelings we wish we did not have. We can only face them, trace down their roots, and put ourselves into the perspective that this new knowledge gives.

One of the hidden dangers of jealousy lies in the psychological system of defense to which it gives rise. Characteristically, a person guards himself against recognizing his own jealousy by unconsciously repressing the inner experiences of jealousy. This means he plunges the twinges of jealousy down into the darkness below the level of his own awareness. He does not even realize what he is doing, so ancient is this maneuver to handle the impulses of jealousy. To push something into the darkness, of course, does not mean to defuse it or to prevent it from having other effects on us. The unconscious in man is not like an attic where the mementos of the past harmlessly collect dust. It is rather the dynamic area which profoundly affects behavior even when we are quite unaware of it.

Jealousy goes quickly underground, in other words, but it still buckles the surface, motivating activities that are expressive of the deep springs of hostility that are blocked from our view by unconscious defenses. In other words, although jealousy operates from the darkness it feeds our daylight behavior and leads us to say and do things to others in a hostile and self-protecting way. We do not, however, have any insight into this precisely because of the repressive nature of our inner defenses. We can feel the pressure of the grip of jealousy and never recognize it because it has been made invisible through the mechanism of repression. When jealousy operates at this level it secretly poisons the springs of love. It spreads rather than eliminates fear, and it closes off instead of opening up our hearts.

Love is something which always urges us to take another step in relationship with others. Love impels us to reach out for the sake of the other person even when the price of doing this may be pain and suffering for ourselves. We work a lifetime at learning to love others in a self-forgetting way, and then we learn that love can even ask more of us. In its final maturity, at the time when love is really the sign of God's life in us, it bids us to see how love for those who are close to us contains an invitation to take a step even beyond these relationships. The fundamental impulse of authentic Christian love touches friends, husbands and wives, whole loving families, and asks that they transform their love from something exclusive to something inclusive. By this I mean that the love of which St. Paul wrote opens us to embracing our neighbors and strangers, to sharing our life and the warmth of our love with them. This is easily said but not easily accomplished.

In fact, we have sometimes so emphasized the exclusive aspect of the love of husband and wife for each other that we have paid little attention to this new dimension of caring which must come into their lives if they are to attain the fullness of love. It is in this completed state of mature love that jealousy is extinguished forever. That is because when we can open ourselves and our love to other persons we are clearly secure enough not to worry that our love might be thereby diminished or lost. It takes a fully grown lover to understand that, in the Christian view of things, lovers cannot live and love only for each other. There is something unfinished about the love of a man and a woman when they have not yet faced the challenge of sharing this love with others.

This challenge can appear in many ways. First of all, it comes in the quite natural way of giving new life, so that children will grow to manhood or womanhood because of the sustaining and nourishing power of their love. This breaks the circle of their one-to-one relationship and gives their love a new routing that forces them to reach out beyond themselves. When their children are born, husband and wife are forever changed in relationship to one another. Those who are eager to justify a new form of marriage in which people will elect to remain childless are not paying enough attention to the ultimately transcendent core of genuine love.

The ultimate challenge of transforming one's exclusive love into something broad and rich that includes others arises in many other ways as well. Any serious Christian, for example, who wants to develop a sense of Gospel community will sooner or later find very hard personal ques-

tions about his willingness to give his love as well as his
time to the project. Building a Christian community is
not an activity as much as it is a new way of living and
responding to other persons under the impulse of the
Spirit of love. The insulated family, turned in on itself
and draining its members for emotional support, finds a
new environment of acceptance and involvement when it
enters a truly Christian community. It is asked to cross
the limits of loving which may have been drawn around its
own members. This is a very difficult thing for people to
do, especially when they are hounded by the jealous fears
that can come to life when they have asked to make both
themselves and their loved ones available for others.

There is a strain involved in the new learning that is
demanded of a couple, for example, who are suddenly
challenged to give each other in some particular way to the
needs of the Christian community to which they belong.
This is a very difficult sacrifice for them to make because
it means the yielding up of private moments which they
had guarded very carefully before. It means many hours
of time and separation from each other may be demanded
if their love is really to be shared with others. It is not
unusual for a husband to feel again the pangs of jealousy
when he is asked to give his wife the freedom to partici-
pate in some work or activity of the Christian community.
This, after all, means a lessening of their very exclusive
way of relating to one another. In many ways, the final
cleansing of jealousy from our lives comes in the atmosphere of the Christian community where we are asked to
commit each other in great trust and faithfulness to the
service of others.

The person who takes the Christian life seriously must
sooner or later consider this challenge to his generosity. He
cannot escape it as long as he keeps himself open to the
action of the Spirit. The measure of a man's religious con-

victions is the measure of his willingness to keep on loving even when its demands, for the sake of others, go beyond what he ever expected. I think of one particular example even as I write this, of a loving husband who spoke to me once of how he had been forced to confront the fullness of his love for his wife, whose activities in behalf of the diocese necessitated frequent absence from home and frequent contact with members of the hierarchy and the clergy. He recognized how much his wife's presence meant both personally and professionally to many of these priests. It was not at first easy, he said, to give his wife to all this; he had never expected that he would have to share her time with so many others. Yet he also recognized that his own love made his wife strong and secure in entering deeply into the special demands of her work. There was suffering in it, yet he knew that the love he shared with his wife radiated effectively beyond them, giving life and hope to others. Their love was a truly inclusive one, demanding more of them, but making them more fruitful as well.

There is probably no area that is more sensitive, that arouses more jealousy, and is less openly talked about than the relationships between adults who are not married to each other. The sociological data of Cuber and Haroff (*The Significant Americans* New York, Appleton-Century-Crofts, 1965) suggest a very high rate of close interrelationships with others on the part of married Americans of the professional class. Ordinary life experience confirms this, although the American male is supposedly quite jealous of any other man taking an interest in his wife. The American male expects more freedom for himself in this kind of situation. In any case, relationships of all kinds abound outside of or alongside of marriage. This question is so complex that it is difficult to sort out all of its aspects with much accuracy.

What is clear, however, is that many of these relationships are immature or reflect the immaturity of the marital relationship in the environment in which they sprang to life. There are cheaters, wife-swappers, and Don Juans, and bored middle-agers looking for excitement. There are also many fairly mature and loving couples who find that the net of their relationships includes some that are much closer than others. Many of these relationships are healthy, the proof that truly loving people can open themselves to other relationships without fearing that their own will fall apart. There is responsible love present in many of them, a love that has moved to include other persons in a wholesome and Christian manner. Indeed, the Gospel message tells us that we must face the implications of such relationships because they can represent an ideal of Christian openness and generous love. Obviously, the world could stand some lessons in the mature management of the close friendships of adults, whether they are married or not. It is precisely in this area that psychological and spiritual growth are imperative if some effective community of friendship and trust is to develop among men. The only long-range way that we can begin to roll back the jealously guarded and hostile borders of prejudice and mistrust is through the creative power of love. This transforming love cannot be restricted to the very narrow world of those men and women who are married to each other. God knows, real love is absent often enough there. But the jealousy that closes men in on themselves, or that triggers the violence of shattered triangles, must be broken at last by some powerful realization of the inclusive nature of real love. This is not creeping up on the world like some cosmic Teilhardian cloud of awareness, joining men in a love they have not struggled for. Indeed, understanding of, much less maturity, in extramarital relationships, is a long way off. And yet, difficult as it is even to conceive,

this is the direction in which the Gospel impulse of love
carries us. Men are meant to be friends with one another,
and only an increase in the generous and inclusive love
that is truly Christian will put an end to jealousy's uneasy
domination of human relationships. The development of
a love that makes us go beyond the furthest limits of our
imagined strength is the love that the Spirit bids us to accept and share with others. This is almost a visionary notion, given the tangle of twentieth-century relationships,
but it is the real work of the Christian community.

The perspective of the Christian's life broadens in the
context of the Christian community. It is in a social setting that his love is challenged to move out even further
into the realms of trust and fidelity that are the essential
qualities of Christian living. The final death of jealousy
comes when man and woman, or friend and friend, are
sure enough of their love that they can entrust each other
to a community of care that goes beyond themselves or
their own family circle. This is the communitarian challenge which constitutes one of the distinguishing notes of
what it means to be a Christian. At the moment when a
man realizes that the challenge to love will take him forever and finally out of himself and ask him to surrender
even those he loves and prizes most, he is redeemed. The
greatest service that the Christian community offers to the
world around it is its profound understanding of and its
willingness to share in the mystery of friendship and love.
This is the essential core of the Christian life, the Gospel
response to the jealousies and fears that mark mankind's
search for real friendship. It does not come in any other
way except through persons who keep widening the circle
of their inclusive love. This is the final goal for all Christians, a mutual sharing in the deepest treasures of their
friendship and the readiness to give this up for other men.

IT IS NEVER BOASTFUL
OR CONCEITED

Love may be blind, but it doesn't live very long if it stays that way. Those who love see and understand more rather than less of each other's true personalities. Because love helps them to see so deeply they can accept and affirm each other in a love that means a sharing of their real selves. Lovers see each other's faults quite clearly, but they can also see deep strengths and the kind of beauty that transcends good looks. Love enables them to see all of this, all of each other as each truly is.

The unfinished nature of love is its secret strength. Love only comes in an imperfect and incomplete way in this life. It is never finished because, of its very nature, love is something alive and so it must grow all the time. Different stages of life merely ask lovers to deepen their love as they learn more about each other. Perfect love is not found, like a statue or a portrait, in some completed form for all to admire. Love is always on the move. If you attempt to freeze it at some moment in time or to hold it static you destroy it. Love is restless to grow, always pushing the lovers beyond their outer limits in learning about and loving each other.

Love is a life's work for those who are touched by it. The man or woman who longs for the perfect lover never finds love at all. The person who waits for a lover who never makes a mistake or who is never a source of even the slightest pain searches for a phantom rather than a real person. The too fussy young girl often ends up as the lonely old maid. Not the least aspect of love's miracle is that it is only found in the relationships of imperfect persons who respond to life's challenge of growth. Love's roots are not set down in the shimmering protoplasm of unformed persons. Love occurs between rough-edged human beings. Love has the power to redeem and to promote growth. When it is real it is always busy accomplishing these ends. Mature love is imperfect love, love that keeps working at getting better as the years go by, love in the only way that it is ever found at all.

It is clear that lovers must bring some identity of their own to their relationship with each other. It is of the essence of love that two separate persons, with differing gifts and differing weaknesses, assert themselves in relationship to one another. Because they are real, even though they are imperfect, something rich and new comes into being. Love thrives on the reality of well-defined personalities who bring the contrast of their differing life experiences into the struggle for unity that is at the core of genuine love. A man and woman who possess a good idea of themselves have the best preparation possible to face the multiple challenges of intimacy.

Love is something that is always just beyond the reach of those people who do not know themselves. These people, who go through life under an identity they have assumed from the outside, are the truly boastful and conceited people, impoverished in their own personality and forever searching for their true wholeness. Not knowing themselves, they frequently pretend that they do as they present a carefully assembled façade to the world. This is made up of their dreams and wishes, but it is unrelated to what they are truly like. These people find it difficult to understand love because they are, consciously or not, still dealing with their own problems of identity. They may seem to be reaching out to others, but they are still reaching for themselves.

This kind of person is stalled at the narcissistic stage of development. He cannot break away from the pool in which his reflection shines back so appealingly. People who are so grossly undeveloped are almost always that way because of a failure in love in those who have been closest to them. This terrible tragedy strikes the children of parents who never really love each other very deeply. A vicious circle develops, the children seeking what they never had at home as they ceaselessly pursue an understanding of themselves which their own home life did not allow them to acquire. In their own marriages they create the conditions in which their children will have the same kind of problem.

These crippled persons manufacture an identity that does not hold up under the pressures of an intimate relationship with another person. They enter rather into pseudo relationships, in which they reach out to a projection of their own selves rather than to another person. They cannot help but seek themselves because they have never really had any hold on themselves. What they present to the other is a form of illusion, a wispy vision made up of their own needs and unrealized wishes. This preoccupation with themselves makes it impossible for them to sense what the other person is really like or to give any love that is really directed to the other. Their own field of vision is blocked by themselves. They are so much in their own way that they never see the other clearly at all. They do not give themselves to the other because they are constantly concerned with finding and supporting their own fragile self-image. Like a group of competitive movie stars on a TV talk show they try to outdo each other for attention. What love there is, is self-directed and grasping, making incessant demands on the other for attention and affection but not really entering into any kind of growth relationship with the other. These are the kinds of occu-

pationally hazardous relationships into which great the-
atrical personalities sometimes fall. Their marriages break
apart because stars are basically too enamored of themselves ever to be able truly to share anything with another.
The narcissistic have a self-contained love affair in which
there is no room for any competitor and, therefore, no
room for any authentic human growth.

The terrible penalty of such inflated self-love is the isolation that comes from their unrealistic expectations. They
have no idea of what love is really like and so they cannot
tolerate the toil and suffering that are so much a part of
sharing life with another imperfect person. The heavily
romanticized version of life just does not have a counter-
part in reality. And so they are always doomed to disappointment, just as they are prey to the demon of jealousy
who is always ready to infect the undeveloped personality.
They are very unhappy people, but they have no idea that
it is the exaggerated picture they have of themselves which
makes it impossible for them to establish a genuine love
relationship. They use the word *give*, but what they act
out is *take*. The sad result of this distorted understanding
of themselves is that they ultimately isolate themselves
from even the possibility of a real human relationship.
This is the inevitable price that is paid by the persons who
cannot move beyond their first love affair with themselves.
The relationships they do make quickly fall apart or are so
fragile that they are hardly nourishing in any substantial
way. These are the relationships of the jet-setters who
restlessly play the game of massaging each other's egos
while they pretend to a style of friendship with each other.
The fast-paced flying from one part of the world to another
distracts them from their uneasiness about the insubstantial quality of what is going on in the heart of their lives.
The same kind of interpersonal isolation is acted out in a
thousand suburbs every day. It is the failure to achieve the

identity that must precede intimacy that sentences so many relationships to failure with the partners clawing at each other instead of sharing life with each other. This produces the loneliness and alienation that are so widespread at the present time. It also breeds the wife-swapping and other games to which the immature turn for self-reassurance.

Uninflated love is possible for people who understand and love what they really are; they have something real to share with others. This kind of love is always imperfect, as has been noted, but it is always fresh and alive too. Life may offer a lot of the same old thing day to day for these lovers, but they respond creatively because of the depth of what they share. People who love this way neither overestimate nor underestimate themselves or each other. They are freed largely from the need for defenses to shore up false pictures of themselves. Grown-up lovers have reached the great goal of being themselves with each other. In the reality of that relationship they can keep on growing and whole new sides of them are opened up through the experience of love. Love that is based on what is real about persons can keep growing. The pseudo love based on images and projections of the self has a short life expectancy.

So much of what is vital to love really centers on the willingness of the loving persons to work hard at understanding each other, even long after they have been married or even after their children have been raised. This essential incompleteness is vital to keeping love bright and active. There is always more growing to be done. It is, in fact, essential to the nature of love that individuals constantly try to refine their sensitivity to one another.

One thinks, for example, of the relationship of author Alan Paton and his late wife. He writes tenderly but very realistically of it in his memoir *For You Departed* (New

York, Charles Scribner's Sons, 1969). It is a story of growth, a hard and painful story at times, but one that reflects the characteristics of so many really loving relationships. Paton had married a widow who continued to wear her first wedding ring. When they had been married some time he experienced a strong attraction to a young woman student. Addressing his wife in retrospect, Paton writes:

. . . You suddenly said to me, *Are you in love with Joan?* And I said, *Yes.* You said, *what are you going to do about it?* and I said, *stop it.* You said, *surely she must be consulted about it,* and I said, *we have already spoken about it.* Then I said to you, *I ask only one thing and that is to go down to Natal and say goodbye to her,* to which you replied, *I am willing that you should.* Later that day, or that night, You said to me, *what did I do wrong?* But I cannot remember what I answered, or if I answered at all. . . . (pp. 104, 105)

Paton went and ended the affair and returned home:

You met me at the door of the house, and you took me into your arms in that fierce way of yours, and you held back your head so that I could see the earnestness in your face, and you said to me, *I am going to make it all up to you.* I do not know when I noticed that you were no longer wearing your first wedding ring, but that night when we went to bed it had gone from your finger. All I know is that when you died I searched the house for it. Strange, is it not, that if I had found it I would have treasured it? It is a strange story altogether, isn't it? But it is a true story of life, and if I lived it again I'd like to live it the same way, only better. (pp. 106, 107)

This catches the flavor of what goes on in a relationship of real love, of how much wrenching suffering may be involved in the process of growth, and of how redemptive for the partners the experience is. This kind of facing a complicated truth together is by no means easy. Yet similar, if less dramatic, challenges fill the calendar of married life. Love that is inflated or conceited would not survive such an experience at all.

This kind of painful but fruitful growth works only for those who have kept their caring from growing cold. There is really no task more challenging for any individual than that of trying to focus consistently on the total personality of the other. This is obviously impossible if you can hardly see the other because there is so much of yourself in the foreground of vision. There is nothing more accurate than the popular description of the unloving person as one who is "filled with himself." A real relationship of love challenges us to break the embrace which we so firmly lock around our own ego so that our arms may be open to others. Lovers spend their whole lives straining to open themselves ever more fully to each other's concerns. The whole redemptive meaning of love is found in the willing effort of lovers to die to the selfishness that is always ready to grow back the minute after we have cut it down. There is really no letup in this, no vacation from the effort that is required, and no turning back once one has entered on the road to sharing life with another.

The meaning of commitment is actually worked out in the day-to-day struggles whose challenge is always the same. Lovers have first to die to themselves in order to give life to each other. The measure of this challenge is only enlarged as husband and wife expand their life together for the sake of the healthy growth of their children. This obviously does not work well in immature and inflated personalities. They can only ooze into the errors of self-deception and self-infatuation that are better called conceit. Love is tougher and stronger than so many of its shallow descriptions. It asks lovers to empty themselves steadily in a thousand commonplace ways for the sake of the other person.

The difficult part about love is that it does not work

unless the man and woman retain their own personalities even as they strive to join themselves in ever closer union with each other. To yield oneself up for the sake of the beloved is not the same as collapsing one's personality in a craven and passive way before the other. It is not to be dominated by the other that one keeps trying to understand what the other is saying, even when the words come half-formed or in the shorthand sighs of troubled feelings. Love is not conquering and being conquered according to a military model of unconditional surrender. Some people may mistake this for love. This caricature is clung to by persons who do not possess their own personalities. Lovers are meant to retain their true differences; that is what makes their loving surrender to each other's concerns so significant. They are themselves and are not diminished through dying to their own concerns in order to respond to one another. Lovers are, in fact, enlarged by this sharing; their own identity becomes more secure even as they are able to share it more deeply. This happens because they cannot truly love without being loved in return. They are thus made whole through their commitment to the dynamic and often painful struggle to give life to one another. This is when they are unconsciously self-forgetful, when their hearts speak to each other, and when their love gives them the strength to face all the other challenges of life without fear.

When people abandon the effort to share their real selves, the lights of love go out in their lives. Here is where so many relationships meet a dead end. It is inevitable for the person whose own distorted view of himself has caused him to place himself, his own feelings, and his own needs always in first place in his relationship with another. When he cannot have his own way, there is no give left, little on which their relationship can continue to develop. At this point estrangement sets in, that cold and aching atmos-

phere in which married people forget their hopes for
friendship and make a separate peace. Their loss is multiplied because they have shut themselves off from the only
dynamic force that gives them real growth. They frequently spend the rest of their time justifying their side
of the difficulty, milking sympathy out of everybody from
business associates to bartenders, but shrunken inside
themselves, sad and undeveloped persons who can only
comfort their own illusions when they have given up the
effort to love.

Real love, then, is based on realism about the self. It
flourishes when two persons who have achieved their own
identities take on the task of a love that continues to ask
them to give of themselves all the days of their lives. At
the same time they will need to preserve their own identities, counterpointing the wonder of their union by the
clear distinctness of their personalities. They will do this
in an imperfect way, making mistakes but redeeming each
other through their ever-present openness to the meaning
of each other. Reality, with all its rough edges, is good
enough for the growth of real love. It doesn't have the
perfection but neither does it have the conceit of an artificial flower. It has something much better, the strength
of life itself.

IT IS NEVER RUDE OR SELFISH

The movers and shakers of the world have always been startled by the paradoxical nature of mature Christian love. The thing Christianity is all about, genuine, freeing love, remains a stumbling block to men who think that "making it" is the meaning of life. To get to the top, to make the fortune, to corner the market: Sentimentality is not high on this list of commercial virtues. But Christianity has always talked about giving everything if you are to gain anything, the mystery of emptying yourself that makes you feel filled, and the willingness to die that makes enough room in you for real life. There is no doubt that organized religion, like any other business venture, has all too often forgotten this essential note of love. And men are never lonelier than when they have mistaken the goals of life and the means to attain them. The fullness of life that comes to those who love is never granted to the competitive or the cynical who live by catch phrases like "Do others before they do you."

Love always brings us back to the same personal point of reference. A man must learn to love himself properly if he is to love others at all. This learning is hard because it demands that he sacrifice himself in the process. The laws of economics or managing mutual funds do not apply to human relationships. Love does not grasp or hold tight to its riches. It is rather openhanded and generous, ready to give freely, knowing that it does not lose anything by giving itself away. Genuine love does not shoulder other people out of the way in order to get first place in the line of life. It makes no headway at all by trampling others down or pushing them aside. Love builds when a man starts moving in the direction that takes him out of himself and toward the service of other people. Love takes root as a man becomes increasingly sensitive to others and to the effect that he has on them. As an individual begins to see himself in an instrumental way, noting that he can either add life to others or take it away from them, he begins to love others more generously. It is this sense of self, this feeling for ourselves as agents of tenderness or pain, that allows us to use ourselves well in the relationships of life. When we are insensitive to ourselves, we can only blunder through life, hurting others even when we do not realize it, leaving the scarred and broken trail that follows always in the wake of rudeness or selfishness.

The 1960s proved to be years in which many of us relearned the original meaning of the word *encounter*. When first used, it signified "to meet an enemy." The encounters of the recent past, both on a social and individual level, put a premium on an assaulting kind of authenticity, and telling it like it is by attacking you as you are. This passion for truth *à la Virginia Woolf* is acted out on many of life's stages: In the protests on the streets and on the campuses, in certain species of group dynamics, and in living rooms and bedrooms all across the land. It is crudeness and selfishness incarnate, and these ravage and destroy human relationships rather than build them up.

Clearly it is a good thing to tell the truth and to establish relationships on the basis of what is real rather than what is false about ourselves. But the truth, as St. Augustine long ago noted, can be "murderous" when it is used as a weapon. In some strange combination of the commercial approach to human relationships, we have reached the age of overkill in confronting each other. Indeed, it is perhaps time to wonder whether all the supposed forthrightness, all the demanded authenticity, have really contributed to better human relationships or not. A man can, after all, use the truth, not to reach another, but to separate himself from another; he can use it to deepen a relationship or to close one off. The truth can make us free, but it can also enslave us to our own inner hostility when it is used merely to overwhelm other people. Honesty is the best policy, but honesty can get lost in our anger, and turn out to be a poor policy indeed. Honesty in dealing with each other demands a seasoning of human understanding and a feeling for each other's weaknesses. We don't have to destroy each other to share the truth lovingly with each other.

The very word sensitivity has, because of the popularity of some styles of encounter groups, almost become a synonym for the exchange of harsh but presumably liberating truth. True sensitivity, however, means being able to see into the world of the other, being able to forgive and take into account the person's weaknesses, offering compassion as much as confrontation. Compassion is just the element that is missing in many contemporary champions of authentic dialogue. Somewhat unforgiving of the human condition, they look on sympathy as a weakness and mercy as a mistake. Psyches stripped raw, personal wounds kept open, weaknesses magnified—these are the elements of the modern-day murderous truth. Why are they this way? Well, it is still true that the best defense is a good offense, as many married people know very well. Attacking others excuses the attacker from the far more difficult business of understanding those he confronts; attack oversimplifies life and masks its complexity; it gives a feeling of power and control to those who use it.

But not everybody can handle the whole truth about himself all at once. Genuine love takes this into account. Indeed, experience in psychotherapy shows that confronting another is a very delicate business. It requires great

skill and sensitivity to whether the other is strong enough
to handle it. Sometimes a premature confrontation closes
off rather than opens up the other person. To confront
too savagely may lead the other to leave therapy rather
than make progress in it. The skilled therapist must be
prepared to stick with the person after the confrontation
in order to help him understand and assimilate its meaning successfully. All this is very different from "hit and run,
take it or leave it, now it's your problem" approach of the
purveyors of murderous truth.

The truly sensitive person is no less committed to the
truth, but he understands that the truth must be shared
in a human manner. Sometimes the other person is just
too weak at the moment to stand another body blow. This
is frequently the case in marriage and family life. A real
concern for fallible human beings makes us put them, at
times, ahead of the naked truth. What is the truth to a
person who cannot yet hear it, or who will not yet lower
his defenses to look at it? What does the savage expression
of truth, the quick slit of the jugular, do to a person who
is just too played out emotionally to handle it? There may
be, along with a time for war and a time for peace, a time
for letting people hold on to their illusions a little longer.
Maybe these illusions are the only things that are holding
them together; maybe these are the only things that they
have left. The Christian tradition speaks of not extin-
guishing the candle that is sputtering low and not breaking the already bruised reed.

I often think of the story a young man told me once of
his father, a wealthy black businessman. It seems that his
father found one of his employees cheating and had to let
him go. A few days later the discharged employee's wife
came to see the boy's father with fire in her eyes. Her husband had not been dishonest, she claimed, it was the boy's
father who was at fault. She went on and on, berating the

man while she stanchly defended her husband. All through it the boy's father listened patiently and tried to indicate how much he understood her concern and her loyalty to her husband. After she had left, the boy asked his father why he had not told her the truth, why he had not produced all the proof of the many thefts of which the man had been guilty. The father replied, "Son, that man is no good and is going to break her heart more. But right now he is the only thing she's got to believe in. What would it do to her to take that away?"

Maybe not many of us can be that understanding or that Christian, especially when we have the proof of how right we are about something. But this man's example teaches us all something about compassion and a needed feeling for each other's weaknesses. If love is never rude or selfish, then the truth, which is such a sensitive part of it, can never be used as a deadly weapon.

Love itself brings enough hurts in the course of any man's life. If we can avoid hurting each other unnecessarily through unwise confrontations we may actually be loving each other a little better. One of the most poignant truths of life centers on the utter vulnerability of lovers to each other.

Of all the sighs of life, none is more heartfelt than the one we humans breathe when we are emotionally hurt by others. Being emotionally offended is a profoundly painful experience, so human and yet so common that everybody knows the feeling firsthand. Most of us put emphasis on the times we have suffered hurt rather than on the times we have been the cause of it. We are, while the breath of life is in us, always on the edge of being involved in it. Hurting and being hurt are combustible elements of the human condition; there is always some danger, but were it absent we would not be human at all.

Some people trade their humanity for insulation from the chance possibility of being hurt. They close their hatches and plunge far beneath life's surface, chasing the shadows of the depths to avoid anyone who seems to them a hunter. They can never get deeply enough away, however, as their own loneliness, like a recurrent fever, reminds them.

There is something infinitely poignant about their defensive maneuvers, just as there is something wrenchingly sad about the testimony they give of themselves. Nobody's cash is as cold as that of the well-known billionaire who, in response to a question about his many marriages, said, "I have always tried to avoid being hurt. It doesn't do you any good, letting a woman get to you that badly. I have been pretty successful at avoiding being hurt, I think." This is a perfect example of how rudeness and selfishness can be marshaled as defenses against the perils that are involved in real loving.

You really give up too much of life, no matter how much you gather in gold, when you try to eliminate hurt totally from your experience. It is only when we can be touched deeply by another that we are open enough to life to understand its meaning at all. That is not an easy thing, despite all that is written these days about the risk of real loving. For, common as hurt is, it is a hard thing to handle. It cannot be ignored and it cannot be laughed off. Sometimes, because of circumstances, there is nothing we can do but feel the pain of it, the throbbing throughout our person that won't go away no matter how we try to distract ourselves.

That is what happens when we are hurt by the person we love most, the one to whom we usually come when emotionally wounded and misunderstood by others. There is no hurt like this one. This misunderstanding, no matter how momentary, cuts so deeply that we cannot even speak without making it hurt more. It is the hurt that can make us back away from each other, from those we trust and hold most dear, as if some cruel fate has suddenly made us into strangers again. Time brings things back into focus, but there are no moments lonelier than those when hurt comes from the ones we love.

The reason for this is clear enough, whether it happens between husband and wife, old friends, or young lovers looking forward to a life together. Love and trust, when they are real, make us lower our guard and open our real selves to others; we are most vulnerable to our beloved, most defenseless with those we love most. That is why the pain is so intense. We do not have any defenses up, nothing to shield us from the blow, no matter how accidentally it is delivered. We can only feel the full force of it, and hear the very breath being knocked out of us at the same time. We can, in moments of such hurt, feel misunderstanding like a hot blade cutting through our innards.

At times like these, times we try to avoid as much as possible, we might think of the fact that this is the way the persons we love feel when we, for one reason or another, hurt them. When we know the measure of such hurt, we may become more careful not to inflict this kind of suffering on others. Much thoughtlessness goes into some of the deepest hurts of life. Nobody really means to hurt the other, especially when the other is near and dear, and yet we go right on doing it all the time, crude and selfish when we would like least to be that way. There are all kinds of cuts, kind and unkind, that we give others without really noticing it. We have to work hard for the maturity that makes us aware of how deadly and hurting our thoughtlessness can be.

There has been a lot of loose talk in the United States lately about how we all share some corporate guilt for this or that event, from assassinations to the generation gap.

It is much easier to make that kind of global accusation against ourselves than to face the real injuries we do quite personally to one another. The latter is hard because we know the sting of hurt and it is not pleasant to think that we can hand the same thing on to others. Some of us even like to feel sorry for ourselves and to nurse our hurts as long as we can. That is why, I think, Christ made so much of wholehearted forgiveness.

There would be no healing for us at all unless we could grant each other real forgiveness. That is not easy because, once we are hurt, we are liable to keep our guard up for a while afterward. But real forgiveness, the Christian element that restores wholeness to people, is given only if we are willing to drop our guard once more. Forgiveness demands that we make ourselves open to getting hurt all over again. That asks a great deal from each of us, much more than a quick *mea culpa* or an embarrassed wish that we would forget that this or that has happened. Forgiveness comes from people who have hurt each other but are willing, out of the love that gives them that awful power still, to run the risk that it may happen again. That is the only remedy there is for the hurts we give to one another.

The scar tissue on lovers' hearts is the sign of the two-edged power of love itself. It is only because love makes us so open and trusting that it also makes us targets for each other's occasional insensitivity. It is through the power of that same love, a gift of the Spirit, that we can bring our faith in each other to even greater fullness. And that is the faith that makes men whole. Love is what holds us together and strengthens us for the hazards of the life in which everybody hurts somebody sometime. We are all responsible for seeing that the human family, full of hurts and aches, experiences more of the loving forgiveness that is written about in the Gospels. Only men who have faced the dangers of the rudeness and selfishness, the saw-

toothed edges of the human condition, can open themselves enough to the Spirit to grow more compassionate as
they become less competitive. Lovers who have learned
this are the ones who transform the face of the earth.

IT DOES NOT TAKE OFFENSE
AND IS NOT RESENTFUL . . .
IT TAKES NO PLEASURE
IN OTHER PEOPLE'S SINS

There are times when we salvage a little pleasure out of the pain of life by warming ourselves over the fires of self-pity or righteous indignation. In fact, some people make this a style of life. They are not so much interested in doing the right thing by themselves or others as much as they are in accumulating affronts. They get a lot of mileage out of these incidents, hauling them up years after they occurred and telling them over and over again in some melancholy celebration of the poor way in which the world has treated them. They are what psychiatrist Karen Horney called the "injustice collectors." They try to win the response of others through the histrionic presentation of themselves as suffering and abused persons.

There are many variations on this theme, and all of them are opposed to the real idea of love. Self-pity leads a person to manipulate other people for affection and attention, which is far different from what characterizes mature love. There are dozens of subtle "games" in which undeveloped and neurotic persons pressure the people closest to them for constant attention and care. They cannot bear for a moment to be without it, and they may make a memorable scene if they do not receive it. Love is not a free kind of sharing for them but rather a whole range of behaviors designed to make secure their neurotic "claims" on other human beings. The manipulator of love is often quite unconscious of the dynamics of his actions. It is a neurotic life style and is not productive of growth either for the individual or for others. Unfortunately, this type of person frequently speaks the language of love, quoting poetic passages of the Scriptures and other works to support his insistent demands on other people. Sooner or later, of course, other people catch on to this style of relationship and back away from it. This merely adds to the manipulator's feeling that he has been treated unjustly and that he has been poorly rewarded for all the good things he has done for others. There is, then, a vicious cycle involved in the relationships of the self-pitying. In their own view of themselves they offer nothing but what Horney has called the "pure gold of friendship." They are very good, then, at feeling betrayed when others do not respond with the massive affection which they feel that they deserve.

The many variations of this theme all spring from the same basic lack of interior growth. What is important to note is that what these people do in the name of love is not love itself. In fact, they give love a bad press, making it a huge oozing and entrapping mass that smothers people to death. There is nothing sadder than the undeveloped person who is still trying to win the love of other people through one or the other techniques that spring from the use of self-pity. I have known lonely old men and women groaning about their uncaring children who have been alienated from them precisely because of their overwhelming demands for attention. I have seen husbands and wives in the prime of life turned away from each other because of the same dynamic. It is all the fault of the other, each tells you, checking off a long list, itemized by some neurotic accounting system, of the injuries that have been suffered. And I have heard lonely old priests who have told the same story of their ill-treatment by others to a whole generation of younger clergy. It is a well-gnawed bone, and yet they worry still, desperately hoping that someone will make up to them for all that they have suffered. There is nothing lonelier than an old man still looking for love.

These people sometimes destroy the lives of those closest to them by turning them into round-the-clock nurses in the intensive-care unit which they have made of their own lives. They nurse their wounds as they curse their fates, wanting mothering more than any real challenge to giving something of themselves. They are something like the grown man I once knew who was very upset after he was married because Christmas could no longer center on him. He still wanted surprises and packages in the same way he had had them as a little boy, and could not comfortably take on the role of giving Christmas away to others. Sadness is enlarged in such lives where there is no room for real love to grow. Sometimes, when these people cannot get enough attention through self-pity, they learn how to play on the guilt feelings of others, making others feel bad as they get even with them through some sure-handed psychological manipulation. This is not far different from the adolescent daydream about how people will revere and miss him once he is dead and gone, the romance of the early death that is so fittingly and fulsomely mourned by others. All these maneuvers do something to others that is the death of real love. Until people can identify and call these things by their right names they can neither love nor be loved with any maturity.

There is something extremely possessive about the manipulator's approach to the question of loving. He must corner the market on the world's love because, after all, he is the center of the universe and other people owe it to him. He is constantly forging manacles and other bonds that will hold people close to him. He does not let himself see what he is doing because he will not lower his defenses long enough to take a good look at himself. He is, however, disfiguring love by making it so totally possessive of the other. In its essential nature, love moves toward non-possessiveness. It aims, even in the most intimate of relationships, to free the other person to discover and achieve his or her own fullness. There is something profoundly redemptive in a love that is, within the limits of the human condition, ordered as much as possible to the welfare of the other.

Now everybody has to learn a lot in order to love in this way, and this is the kind of wisdom we learn only the hard way. Yet this is the face of grown-up love. Nothing less than this can possibly give or sustain people through a lifetime together. It is by no means easy to love another and, at the same time, respect the other enough to allow him to be separate from us. You cannot give this gift of free and full life to another unless you put to death the selfishness that makes you want to claim the territory of the other as solely your own. A man dies a lot in a lifetime of respecting the other enough to free him to pursue what is right and appropriate for his own life. This demand is so common it is strange that lovers should be surprised to find it ever present in their lives. True lovers belong totally to each other only when they still prize each other's freedom and individuality.

At the heart of any real love there is a growing core of non-possessiveness, an increased willingness to care for the other mostly for the other's sake. This is as good a barometer as we have of whether people really love each other. We get better at this as we open ourselves to the Spirit of love through overcoming the neurotic inner urges to love others for what we consciously or unconsciously get out of it. This willingness to allow the other his or her separate existence is not incompatible with the kind of possession of each other and freedom with each other which real lovers understand and cherish. In fact, the sense of being comfortable with each other, the deep sense of belonging totally while remaining separate, this serene sense of trusting one another completely: These grow and develop only as lovers learn the hard lessons of freeing each other rather than manipulating or using each other. It is the calm clear landscape, full of peace and joy, into which lovers move after they have struggled together through the dark thickets in which they love themselves more than each other.

When a person reaches this stage in understanding the meaning of love, he also begins to understand that real lovers even respect each other enough to know when to leave each other alone. Actually, the catalogue of misfortunes inflicted by humans on each other in the name of love is very large. Throughout the course of history people have done the most astounding things to each other, always with the energetic reassurance that the sole motive for the action was love. This begins early with large spoonfuls of bitter medicine held firmly in reportedly loving parental hands; doctors and dentists lulling us into an innocent vulnerability with promises that "This won't hurt a bit"; the father of the family administering some heavy-handed discipline to a soft-bottomed child with the unlikely protest that "This hurts me more than you."

It is a part of wisdom to understand that people who love each other must allow each other to suffer at times. Life must be faced, and the pain is made tolerable only because someone else does love us and supports us through it, even when he or she cannot prevent it. This understanding is found between husbands and wives, and between them and their children; friends know this experience as well. It is not easy to let someone you love suffer a crisis of growth, an illness, or a trying experience at school or at work. But lovers face these things all the time and redeem each other through entering into them together.

Far different from this, and distinctly non-redemptive, are the people who move into the lives of others with plans for remodeling them. Like amateurs who try to remodel anything, they are confused about their purpose, their motivation, and their skills. They frequently end up causing a good deal of damage. This is exactly the case with the meddler who flies the banner of love as he charges into the inner precincts of another person's personality. He calls his destructive foray by the name of love, and he manifests his misunderstanding of love in a wide variety of situations. You see it in the busybody who has plans for your perfection and is always willing to share them with you. There is the person who has long-range plans for your life and attempts to force them on you. Widely assorted are the individuals who want you to respond emotionally to them and who manipulate you, even to the quoting of Scripture, to get you where they want you. Familiar, too, are the enthusiasts for some particular form of prayer or supposedly spiritual experience who absolutely insist that you join them. Worst of all, I suppose, is the individual who inserts himself into the relationship of two other people with the supreme self-confidence that his loving intervention will help the others to be better in some way or other.

There is no denying the usefulness of friends who are truly interested in us and who do love us enough to confront us with either our shortcomings or our unfulfilled possibilities. That, however, is not the kind of friend I am describing here. The meddler can be easily recognized for several reasons. First of all, he is basically insensitive to himself and to other people. He has a short supply of insight to match his ardor for interfering with others. Most prominent in his make-up, although perhaps unsuspected by him, is the role his own needs play in his relationships with others. He is not seeking the good of the other nearly as much as the satisfaction of some drive or need of his own. He will not admit this, of course, and to cover it he invokes the notion of love. This is why he is so harmful to others; he gives love a bad name because of his superficial understanding of it. He has not learned the first lessons of loving. He is a world away from the respectful love that sets others free.

The core difference between the meddler and the lover lies in the selfishness of the former and the selflessness of the latter. A real lover puts himself and his own needs to death for your sake. The lover reaches out, but the meddler closes in. The lover, even when he is leaving you to your own pain, prizes you: The meddler, even as he may be causing you pain, is first in his own affections.

The meddler and the manipulator are first cousins to each other, superficial, selfish, and basically unloving, despite their rhetoric. They end up living life sentences in the solitary confinement of their own souls. They don't tell us much about real love, except through showing us the emptiness and meanness of lives in which it is lacking. Real love is much harder and, of course, more rewarding than these neurotic imitations. It is, as St. Paul says in comparing with other gifts, "better than any of them." There is no room for self-pity in the lives of real lovers; they are too busy learning more about each other and the sacrifice that goes into freeing each other to have any spare moments for feeling sorry for themselves. They know the great Christian secret of genuine love endures: Loving demands dying, and emptying the self leads to a fullness that the self-pitying can never even imagine, much less understand.

IT IS ALWAYS READY
TO EXCUSE, TO TRUST, TO HOPE,
AND ENDURE WHATEVER COMES

These words of St. Paul sum up some of the most powerful aspects of human experience, the things we know in our bones make us human, the things without which we are not much more than naked apes mating and feeding away in the human zoo. These actions of love that is alive tap the reservoirs of our humanity, bidding us to risk everything to bring our real selves into the daylight of life with other people. Love excuses, trusts, hopes, and endures only when men and women stop holding back and give themselves over fully to these basic human tasks. The fundamental meaning of life and the fundamental meaning of religion are to be found in the lives of persons who strive to trust and believe and support each other through hard times. What the Spirit works in us does not take place on the mountaintop or in the desert. His bright wings beat over the earth only where men are trying to love each other truly.

There is something that fits together in the things that are really human and the things that are divine. There is no arbitrary border line between the sacred and the secular where living and breathing human beings are concerned. What is truly human is what is touched by the Spirit. It is only in the things that are human that the Spirit is revealed. The work of the Spirit is best seen, then, in what is best in man. And man is called upon to give his all in love much more than in any other activity. People have written cynical caricatures of love, and the immature have presented fragile and insubstantial visions of it. It can sometimes seem weak indeed, the opposite, as it were, of strength. Such are the visions, for example, of those who hold that love is passivity, a holding back from life. This is the mistranslation of love that is invoked by many people who wish to escape the very real challenge of loving because they are not strong enough to take on the task. They say, behind their banners and flowers, that they would like to be taken care of and that they would like to escape pain insofar as this is possible. They want to have good feelings, a sense of community, and who cares if marijuana helps this all along a bit? This kind of passivity is ultimately self-defeating because it isolates the individual from love even as it inoculates him against the pain of reality.

Deceived as well are those who think that love means doing your own thing and letting everybody else do his own thing, no matter how disorderly, disruptive, or self-hating this may in truth be. Acceptance must be absolute with no questions about whether one could do better or whether there is a richer potential self just waiting to be born. Everybody stays at a certain distance, making no demands, having no hopes, insured against the disappointments of believing in each other by letting everybody go his or her own way. This is an extraordinary defense against the complexity of loving despite all the contradictions, shortcomings, and deceits that are part of everyday life. This total acceptant definition of love is an exaggeration of the acceptance that really is a part of genuine love. It is a distortion that eliminates the boundaries of reality, eliminates a sense of responsibility, and offers a psychedelic kind of narcissism.

The saddest part about these misunderstandings of love is that the really good news about love is so much better than any of these distortions. It is much more demanding, much harder, but much more productive of growth and peace and joy. The publicists who deceive the young into accepting one of these undeveloped ideas of love are short-changing these people and deceiving them cruelly. They are not helping them to face and understand the true dimensions of human relationships or the discipline that is required both to love yourself and to love anybody else. The person who thinks that love is mere gentle passivity or some kind of disengaged acceptance will find that trust and hope are a great drain on his strength. The young who have not been helped to understand the fundamental characteristics of friendship and love will find it hard to meet the tests of love when these arrive in their lives. And one thing is certain: These tests wait for everybody, no matter how carefree or protected from life they may now seem.

Real love excuses the other because it has a feeling for the imperfect nature of human existence. A real lover can excuse his beloved precisely because he loves the other in reality and not in some idealized state. A wife, for example, can look deeply into her husband's life and understand, in a way that no one else could, why he behaves as he does. She knows all the secret hurts, the sensitive spots, and even the potential as yet unrealized. She can take all this into account, and instead of standing outside of him and judging him harshly, she can add her strength to his, not by rationalizing away his faults, but by joining in his struggle to grow a little more every day. The same thing works for the husband in relationship to his wife. He knows the inner landscape of her personality. Love bids him to keep exploring it with her, making his strength gently present, putting himself fully at her side with the sensitive understanding of all the things that make her the way she is. This kind of effort to understand, to reach out and look with compassion into the world of the other, is at the heart of any kind of love that wants to last very long. This is an everyday kind of a task, not something done once a year to clean off the slate, but a redemptive exercise in which warmth and understanding make up for all the faults and strains that can be found between all lovers.

Unless understanding is regularly exercised, the failings only pile up, clogging the communication, and breeding the poisons of growing hostility that have the power to kill love off. People who love each other know that there is a lot about each of them that needs understanding. That is one of the chief things they look for in each other. If lovers do not have this sort of understanding for each other, then the days of their love are numbered. Understanding is a very powerful ingredient in human relationships; it is as indispensable to man's survival as water and food. But it is hard work constantly to be willing to listen to and to look deeply into the other with the compassion that is motivated by real love. It is, however, just what lovers do for each other in order to help each other to grow to full maturity.

To understand another person is life work enough for a real lover because human beings are never exhausted of their richness. There is always something new to learn, something around the corner of the other's smile or frown that waits to be discovered. Only people who *respect* each other in the profound meaning of that word, who can *look again* at each other and see something richer and deeper each time, have an appreciation for understanding as a component of love. Life does not get boring for people who are gently open and receptive to each other. I think, for example, of the lady married nearly fifty years who told me recently how many new things she had learned about her husband only after he had retired from business. And something of that spirit of discovery and enjoyment of each other clearly marks their marriage. That reciprocal

* Endless wonder for the other

affirmation of each other through the increased sharing born of understanding is one of the fruits of working at love. It is, in a humanly observable form, one of the ways people resurrect each other through the gift of love.

This kind of sensitive understanding, this joyful interplay of growing personalities, does not come out of the blue or because of the convergence of the stars. It is what happens, however, when people work at loving each other and when they are ready to die to themselves in order to live for somebody else. This orientation to the other, this willingness to reach out in love, catches the meaning of redemption in human experience. The initiative of Christian love constantly goes out to the other even before the other has made any response at all. This, as psychologist Father Charles A. Curran has so thoroughly developed in his books, is a genuine religious act insofar as it parallels God's love, which came to us while we were still sinners. This "loving first" is a characteristic of redemptive understanding love, a response through the Spirit to the value of the other, which we grasp only if we open ourselves to it. In practical language, we understand only when we stop thinking solely of ourselves and can begin to focus on others around us. That calls for a steady transformation of ourselves through the power of love. But it hurts even as it gives new life, and some find it too hard really to continue. They end up as the searchers, longing for the mysterious touch of assured love, but incapable of the self-sacrificing initiatives of understanding that alone make it available for us.

For love to flourish, we have to do something about it. This is precisely where the misinterpretation of love as passivity betrays people into an expectant inactivity which renders them incapable of the understanding, trusting, and enduring that show that love is alive.

Believing and trusting another person are hard work

too, the most hazardous and exhausting known to man. These are the signs of how different man is from other living beings. He is aware, and deepens his awareness as he grows up, of the personal cost of these experiences. To hope and to believe in other persons: We do these only when we spend ourselves in the process. Trusting and sticking by another person means putting our undefended selves on the line in the area of life where we make the best targets. The price is always the same, and it can only be paid by those whose motivation comes from the Spirit. The deepest questions of life, the issues that are of greatest significance to persons, always center on the vulnerability of the human heart in the adventure of love. Hurt is a certainty even in the deepest loves; it is as much a part of the pattern of loving as the need to die to ourselves is of the pattern of living. Man's strength, his real strength rather than any assumed image of strength, is tested through the long moments of waiting and longing that go into trusting another. The moments when his strength is thus engaged are also the moments when his real personality most fully emerges. The moments of holding on, of believing in people who can disappoint us, of letting our children learn their first lessons of responsibility on their own, of remaining true to our beloved when distance keeps us apart: These are the moments of heightened experience in which we feel most keenly what is demanded of us when we love. There is small wonder that we can be so easily tempted to turn aside from the disciplined involvement, the holding of ourselves in place in relationship to others that believing and hoping require of us. And there are many good-sounding arguments we could muster up to excuse ourselves from the constant tension of loving. There are probably more plausible-sounding rationalizations available to us now than ever before. Faithfulness is indeed a good example of this.

The present climate of our country offers little encouragement for the faithful person. Indeed, the man who tries to keep his commitments as best he can must get discouraged at times when he sees infidelity, in so many forms, rewarded. The non-hero, the adulterer, the deserter; we have found reason to praise them all of late. The real question must be: Why are men faithful in a culture that fails to reward it?

It is not easy to remain faithful to one's wife, one's responsibilities, or one's convictions, when the world makes it easy for us to put them aside. There are many signs of this, for example, in connection with marriage. Recently, in books and articles, we have seen an increasing emphasis on the positive aspects of infidelity. An affair outside marriage, some people say, is good for the marriage, or at least good for you, and not necessarily harmful to the marriage, especially if the other partner does not know about it. So, too, moralists are becoming more tolerant of infidelity and are saying so publicly, even as they note the danger of generalizing about such matters. Lawyers have come to the concept of the "no-fault" divorce, so that adultery is fast disappearing even as a legal entity. Add to this the reported change in the attitude of women about these concepts and one can understand the pressure the person who struggles to be faithful must feel.

Much of the glorification of extramarital adventures comes from clever but superficial minds. Publicists and *Playboy*-minded philosophers of the good life do not have to pay the price for the kind of behavior which they encourage in others. Neither do other social observers or moralists who, on frequently shaky kinds of data, find good things in unfaithfulness. They are removed from the anguish of everyday life, and they seem at times quite insensitive to the widespread signs of man's longing for some affirmation of faithfulness. This comes across, among

other places, in the women's magazines, where hardly an
issue appears that does not contain one or more articles
that express a woman's uneasiness about the faithfulness
of spouses in marriage. It comes across in the cries of
youth who are searching, as much as for anything else, for
some adults in whom they can truly believe. They protest
an elder generation's infidelity to itself and its commitments. That is why the key word in their slogan about
those over thirty is "trust." It is hard for them to trust
people whose behavior seems to them to be marked by
too many sellouts to forms of infidelity.

It is striking that the world has so little to say that is
positive about the concept of faithfulness. Perhaps it has
lost hope because it has known so much in the way of disappointment. It is surely here that Christians have something to say and something to show to the world. If, as
psychiatrist Leon Salzman has noted in his extensive research on infidelity, there is always some failure of commitment, some lack of real love involved, it is clearly a
Christian obligation to offer a better understanding of
these things to mankind. Underneath all the glorification
and pseudosophistication, infidelity flourishes where people have forgotten how to love each other and have given
up the sometimes difficult work of staying in love with one
another.

The Christian who tries to live by the Gospels offers
the world some insight into what is demanded of those
who would spend a lifetime together. Love, when it is
understood as a process of growth that includes joys and
pain, is a distinct challenge to the concepts of instant
gratification and "Let's not make any claims on each
other" that are currently fashionable. The most revolu-
tionary thing a Christian could stand for is not a bloody
uprising against the establishment, but a real belief in the
meaning of love. That is not easy, because it demands that

people continue their search of themselves and of each other, that they continue to listen and to grow in relationship with each other, even as age and circumstances work great changes in them. It is getting easier all the time to give up when a relationship finds itself in difficulty. People who buy this philosophy gradually find that there is no center of gravity in their lives, that their identity is a smear, and that their restlessness is not quieted by all the mood music culture plays to practice infidelity by.

If Salzman's assessment of his clinical experience is correct, then it is more important than ever to preach the Gospel message to others. Perhaps Christians need a few words of encouragement that they are on the right track when they continue, under the guidance of the Spirit, to believe and trust and suffer through things with each other. Our greatest infidelity is our faithlessness to the world when we lost confidence in the saving power of the Gospel and the values which it offers still to men.

When we come right down to it, the Gospel values and the things that make man different from the animals overlay and intermingle with each other in the responsibility with which we meet the demands of intimacy. It is in the way we possess ourselves and give ourselves to each other that we encounter life and the life of the Spirit as well. The demands of religion do not pull us away from each other to worship a God who will have nothing to do with our love for each other. The real test of faith is not in whether we accept a certain set of intellectual statements that interpret the cosmos for us. It is rather in that confrontation with ourselves (which we can hand over to no one else) in which we measure our willingness to accept the personal demands of believing, trusting, and enduring, that the Spirit of love urges on us. Nowhere else in our experience will we have to face so clearly the redemptive character of loving. We enter into a relationship in which only death to self leads us on to the full life of resurrection. It is a never completed sequence, recurring as it does over and over in the thousand settings of human love. We may be able to talk around love or talk about it at times—but when it comes to belief and hope we cannot use the escape of words. We either actively embrace these aspects of love, and discover life as we discover each other, or we lock ourselves out into loneliness because the price is too high. And that makes all the difference between being alive and existing, between knowing something of the miracle of being human or being destroyed because the love we need for life has been denied us.

There are only illusory distinctions between trusting and hoping and enduring. They are really part of the same response, and you cannot give the one without giving them all. The world falls apart when men run out of their supply of understanding and trust or when, in a last desperate state, they give up believing in these things at all. The task for the man who is truly religious is to care enough to keep these elements of love alive for the rest of mankind. That begins in his own life but clearly cannot end there. Faith and hope as parts of love open us to our Christian responsibility to share the good things of God's love with everybody. There is no real religious belief, practice, or celebration when an understanding of these things is absent.

You can write a great deal more about these qualities of love and still not write enough. What a man needs to do is to open himself to love by putting aside his defenses against it. It will inevitably come into his life if he doesn't lunge after it. Then he will experience the fire of the Spirit that is meant to light up the whole world. And he will understand, in the experience for which words can never substitute, the whole meaning of the Christian life.

IT DOES NOT COME TO AN END

Men turn their collars up against what Albert Camus called the "dark wind" of death. Its mystery and its secrets seem intolerable; man shouts at it, demanding an explanation, and silence is his only answer. Man attacks it, trapping it with scientific advance, keeping it a little longer at bay with better food and better housing, or seducing it with cosmetic transformation. And yet, no matter how far he extends the road of life and no matter what reprieves he buys, death still stands waiting for him.

Death is an unacceptable reality in a world where men see it only as an enemy to be overcome at last. But death cannot have that meaning for somebody who has experienced real love. And so death cannot be a final cold stillness for any Christian who is really alive. Indeed, there is only one power that outlasts death, and that is the power of love. Great mysteries come together in the subject of death, and only when man is strong enough to look deeply into it, can he look back at life with real understanding. Man knows a thousand kinds of death, from the helplessness of watching the sun go down on a happy day to the uncomfortable awareness of what aging does to his physical powers. Everything worthwhile slips away even as man tries to hold on to it. In the same way he senses that the seeds of death are already sown into every living thing. There is a sharp edge to life's reality. And on that sharp edge are met some of the related truths about love and death.

Love and death are by no means strangers to each other. Love is shot through with the images and echoes of death.

There is the death to self that precedes and strengthens authentic love as well as the death that lovers know because they can never share enough of life together. The redemptive quality of love depends on the willingness of lovers to accept the partial deaths that so fill their lives. And in this resides one of the deepest mysteries of Christian love. Far from being the mindless togetherness to which some aspire, love is filled with separation and hints of death. This is incomprehensible except against the pattern of the life of Christ, which is the model for the resurrected life of every Christian. Those who will not face and deal with the inevitability of separation and death in everyday life misunderstand love and try to make of it something which it can never be. Every real lover knows that loneliness and pain are a part of intimacy that cannot be cut away without killing love itself.

Indeed, lovers know a special loneliness. This comes at the many times when they must be apart, or in the moments when they realize how much they want to share and how limited they are in ever sharing completely the best things in the human condition. Real lovers are not lonely because they are not loved; they know the unique mystery of separation that is heightened precisely because they are loved deeply. Some of the mystery of those who love each other echoes through the Gospels. Christ separates Himself from His family, He draws apart from His friends, He allows Himself to feel deep loneliness in the Garden of Olives, and He baffles His Apostles when He reveals that the necessity of His leaving them is intimately bound up with His redemptive mission. Christ's departure from His closest friends is necessary if the Spirit is to come to them. "You are sad at heart because I have told you this. Still, I must tell you the truth; it is for your own good that I am going because unless I go, the Advocate will not come to you; but if I do go, I will send him to you."

The climax of Christ's life, in His crucifixion and death, is a shattering moment of separation as He leaves His loved ones humanly desolated. It is this moment of separation, when Christ allowed Himself to feel so alone and uncomforted by the Father, when His mother and friends were left to know the depths of loneliness, this moment of separation of Christ's Body and Blood is the one remembered in the Eucharist. Each experience of personal aloneness or separation from those he loves reflects the Christian's participation in the ongoing redemption of the world.

This element of separation even in the midst of the most profound love is inescapable. When it is not the separation that is merely the product of indifference or hostility that creep into marriage to kill love off, it is an indispensable aspect of a truly loving relationship. We have been blinded to the dynamic and redemptive significance of separation as a part of love because of the effect of clichés about absence making the heart grow fonder. We have also looked on it more as an evil to be rooted out than a realistic fact of life. There is a real mystery here into which only true lovers can enter, a mystery of life in the Spirit that draws people close and asks them to bear in faith the deaths of a thousand separations. It is the mystery of salvation through the kind of trusting and confirming love that enables lovers to bridge the gaps in their lives with a sense of sureness about their love that transcends the moments they are apart.

Life together is what lovers long for, the constant and intimate delight in each other's presence that is the unselfconscious play of true affection. But life repeatedly separates lovers, even husbands and wives, through work, household chores, and the shifting schedules of growing

children. They frequently find that their moments together are fewer than they wish; they can either enter
into the reality of life that asks them to give each other
away constantly to the needs of others, especially their
children, or they can rebel against the constant demand
on their generosity. The last strategy has many faces:
Sometimes it looks like selfishness, a withdrawal from life,
and sometimes it is an almost overwhelming draining of
lovers' strength as they try to be the sole source of emotional support to each other. The burden of turning away
from the element of separation in love becomes heavy
indeed. In fact, it is a source of breakdown for many relationships. People just demand too much of each other,
forgetting that love involves them necessarily in a world
wider than themselves, one in which they will have to die
constantly in order to preserve and grow in their love for
one another. And the only means to ensure growth together is a willingness to pay gladly the price of sharing
their love. Love is too good ever to be kept clutched closely
to one's breast; that makes it seem like some foolish
treasure that might be stolen or lost. Real love grows as
people face the death to themselves that making their
love available to others always entails. When lovers can
embrace the absences, the separations, the giving away of
each other that genuine love requires, then they have
joined themselves to the action of Christ's redeeming
sacrifice. What Christ did was not distant, something hard
to remember, or only symbolically re-enacted in the
Eucharist; it is for lovers the very reality of going through
life together, the sacrifice that makes sense of all their
sacrifices, the laying down of life that overcomes separation and death forever. Lovers know the meaning of the
Eucharist because it permeates their own everyday
struggles, making them aware of how intimately they live
in Jesus when they accept the invitation to lay down their

lives for each other in love. It is through lovers that the redemption of the world is carried on.

Life is filled with impossible loves, with people who have had to reach across chasms of separation to support and sustain each other. Some of the deepest and most responsible love that I have seen in this life has been mysteriously present outside of marriage. I have seen it in the lives of priests and religious who have struggled with the basic meaning of redemptive love in trying to understand their role of service to a wider family than one of their own. I have seen it in people kept apart by illness or other obligations of caring for sick relatives—lovers who have had to face unexpected sacrifices for the sake of others. And I have seen, in the complexity of real life, men and women reach across the boundaries of marriage itself to give support and strength to others without breaking the vows of either marriage. I have seen love like this, a love seldom written or spoken about, but a love whose source is in the Spirit, and it is a love which gives life as it gives everything and can take nothing in return.

Not many people can love so deeply because not enough people are mature enough to face up to the ultimate demands of accepting the gift of love in their lives. These are the people who need others to help them understand love better and to help them to grow in sharing it with others. Quite simply, that is one of the chief functions of any community that calls itself a Church: To create the environment in which people can grow up enough to love each other more truly and more responsibly. The Church is meant to preach the dynamic of redeeming love, of that power that illumines the commonplace of everyday life, and that integrates all the loose ends and suffering of human lives. Love that understands separation is also love that overcomes death. It is in the experience of this kind of love that you get a hint of immortality, because such love is stronger than all separation and all barriers, even the seeming high wall of death. It is not only the fact that separation is so much a part of love that tells us this. There is something else in our experience that gives us some insight into the transcendent meaning of love.

A promise of immortality springs from the fact that love lasts. We have never taken this truth as seriously as we should. Love endures, carries on its effects in us, and continues to be powerful well beyond the moment or the relationship in which it is experienced. Love is not like food that provides temporary nourishment but does not permanently stay the rhythm of hunger. Love gives us strength that remains with us because it adds something to us that does not ebb away of itself. It changes us because it makes us grow and there is no going back on growth that has been achieved. Love that we have really known from another lives on in us even when the other has left us through death or separation. It is like a fire in us that burns brightly to light our way and warm us for the days when we are alone or under stress. It kindles our own motivation and our own power to love; we can keep giving love away without losing any of it.

We think about love in very limited ways, and we are too intimidated by the songs and stories that speak only of the desperate fear of losing love. We even limit the possibilities of experiencing it when we are so dominated by the fear of its slipping out of our grasp. That is not the way of real love, which is made of far more durable material. It is, however, the way of the many inadequate and substitute notions of love that plague us. That is the love we try to demand of another as an account payable, or the wisp of love that is merely a passing attraction or the echo of our own need.

There is a great mystery about real love that has never been captured by poets, artists, or sentimental preachers.

It is solid and deep, a miracle far more common than visions, or wonders, a wonder in itself that cannot be bartered or put safely away, like gold, in some cool private vault of our personality. Love does not seek a hiding place; it demands expression and it craves sharing with others. Genuine love is active, its dynamism undiminished by the passing of years or the shifting of circumstances. It is, of its essence, creative, and so it gives and sustains life. It wants to be out in the open where it can grow and spread to others.

Christians, least of all, can view love as a perishable commodity, or as something that must be locked away from life itself. And the most unacceptable notion of all, if we take the Gospels seriously, is that love is dangerous. It is powerful, yes, but it is not dangerous. It flourishes in those who can face the problems of loving and the hurts that life can inflict. The real danger exists for those who never want to face these things and who never experience any real love at all. It is a strange thing that so many Christians are shy about loving and so unwilling to open themselves to it, or to let others open themselves to it. They choose rather to build walls and fences against the supposed dangers of love, and so they do not know the moment of love or its continuing power. They are the lonely ones who will not let themselves understand that real love casts out the haunting danger to all life, fear.

There is a mystery in love because it breaks down walls and topples over fences. It does not confine itself to one relationship or one style of relationship. Love is found in many places, and we would not be afraid of it if we really believed in the Gospels. This is true because any love that is selfless is the work of the Spirit, the action of God in our lives, the evidence we can know that supports our faith and our hope. Because it is the sign of God touching our lives, it is powerful and creative. As philosopher Robert Johann has written, those who have loved have been given "a glimpse of the world beyond care."

The most distinguishing mark of lasting and creative love is found in the sense of responsibility that goes with it. This is far different from the hit-and-run tactics of those who use other people for a while and then put them aside. It is a world away from those who play at loving others with glowing phrases and a mastery of the manipulative arts. It is meant to last, and so it imposes a telling discipline of its own, a discipline that flows from a sense of being responsible for the other in season and out. This means that a real lover is committed to the good of the other and not just to the satisfaction of his own need. It suggests that a genuine lover wants the beloved to grow; only the counterfeit lover wants to control the other in all the aspects of life.

The lessons of loving are not mastered all at once. Sometimes it takes a lifetime of learning and perhaps we must settle for the human condition of getting better at it as the years go by. This, too, is one of the effects of real love because it matches the way men are and helps them to continue the process of growing out of themselves. That is why love lasts and enables us to learn to share it even with our enemies. The Gospels tell us all of this, just as they tell us that it is never too late to respond to the Spirit of love that can so transform our lives.

It is often the remembered moments of love that keep us going beyond the imagined limits of our own strength. When love is real it is powerful in the mark it makes on us. It enlarges us and moves us always forward. Love's inherent strength makes it more powerful than death or any of the hazards of life itself. Love is what Christians should be good at, so that the whole world can be strengthened to put away its fears.

Men have always wanted to leave something lasting behind themselves. Only the mighty or the highly gifted have the chance to do this through history or the arts. Everyone, however, leaves something that outlasts the greatest fame or accomplishment when he reaches out, even for a few moments, in loving another. He touches the ways of all men and their destiny when he can love one man with deep responsibility. He becomes an instrument of life, ever-increasing life, when he truly loves. His name may be forgotten, but the presence of the Spirit survives in the love he leaves behind.

A TIME FOR LOVE

Man has never described the nature of time very well. Insights have been provided by philosophers and physicists, but none of these has ever explained the mystery of the passing minutes. Americans seem to favor the economic theory of time. After all, time is money, we say, and we want to spend it well. It can be invested, and with care and a good retirement plan, it can be redeemed with interest in later years of leisure. Time is a condition as much as anything else for us; if there is one thing we want as a condition of most of our activities, it is that they be performed fast. And faster the next time around, if at all possible.

So we have a passion for fast cars and fast planes; we long for short cuts in cooking, baking, and putting things together; we lap up speed reading, digests, and review books that let us pass tests on the great works of literature without ever needing to take the time to read them. The great virtue is whether we can save some time by buying this or doing that; in fact, the factor of speed, as found in TV dinners and franchise foods, makes up for what may be lacking in quality.

Only now are men beginning to question the technology that has saved so much time in so many different ways and yet generated greater problems in the process. Speed whets man's appetite for more speed, and he long ago passed the point where the diminishing returns set in. For man is restless with all his saved time, vaguely guilty at not having something purposeful to do, or, groggy from the collapsed time zones of jet travel, he is uneasy and awkward about how to use the leisure in his life. Other cultures seem to have a much less compulsive set of feelings about time. They may be driven by other demons, but they are driven at a little less headlong pace.

Time, no matter how we define it, is not used up by doing things faster. Indeed, postmodern man, for all his hurrying, knows that his real problem is filling his time in a humanly fitting way. The problem of meaning, the problem of man's understanding of himself and his goals; the dimension of time enfolds them all. And time is something that the prophets of the postindustrial world tell us we will only have more of in terms of leisure and life expectancy. But what does man do with his time? Leisure is still a monstrous puzzle for everyone nurtured on the Protestant ethic. And anomic man, still searching for the values that give meaning to time, is shuffling around, getting ready to put out the lights of the twentieth century. He is stunned already by yet another face of time, the future. He can make out its shape against the dawn of the next century, and he is already anxious about what he will be like and what he will do after the year 2000.

In the meantime, with one anxious eye on the clock, man wonders why breaking the time barriers has not made him happier. He finds himself still a victim of time, regretting the past, worried about the future, and unable to grab hold of the present. Where, he wonders, did all the time go, or all the flowers, or the chances, or the quickly growing children? These are difficult questions, the ones that get into the heart of a man, and make him search for a center of gravity in a world that is moving too fast all around him.

One of the realities of life that has suffered from our commitment to speed is the very thing that man needs if he is to get the time of his own life into perspective. That, of course, is love. And how many time-related questions man can ask about that! How long, real lovers ask, have we loved each other? And have we changed as time has gone by? Was there ever really a time when we were not waiting for each other? And why should love stand the test of time, in a world where so few other things do? Man has dozens of such half-formed questions on the edge of his consciousness. He has not, however, taken the time to speak them clearly, even to himself.

The accelerated pace of life, the seldom questioned conviction that doing things swiftly is the same as doing them well: These make time press like a weight on us and make us miss or distort the values of love that need time to grow and develop. Love needs time. There is just no way around it. Despite our talk of whirlwind courtships and love at first sight, real love cannot take root unless it has time to do it. Love needs time even for those lovers who recognize something in each other the first moment they meet. They need time to test it and to test themselves as well. The old tradition of courtship recognized this just as it understood the wisdom there is in waiting for things.

The idea of ever waiting for anything good, that is, of delaying gratification, is thought to be the raving of a deluded person at best these days. And yet, the ability to wait, and to make sacrifices while waiting, are components of genuine love that cannot be put aside as though they were of no account merely because they seem to be out of fashion. One of the most severe problems for a generation that has been encouraged to grab at whatever it wants and to pay it off on the installment plan, is precisely the human problem that life with other people does not work well that way. It is easy to exempt man from the rhythms that link him in a thousand ways to time and place in a world that turns too slowly for him. The jet plane, as we have mentioned, shortens his journeys but throws him out of phase with the internal clocks that relate him to the moods and pace of nature in the place he calls home. In a world growing keenly aware of the word ecology, man is discovering that he is not himself immune to the demands of keeping in some balanced relationship to his surroundings. He fits into the world that is always half shadow and half light, and he dislocates himself, in the name of speed, only to find that nature takes a measure of revenge that he cannot escape.

It is the same way with love. The element of time cannot be put aside as though it had no relevance to the emotional ecology of growing human relationships. But the deep and hard-bought wisdom of how much waiting or separation go into the development of love is not popular with people who want everything here and now. There are consequences for a person when he exempts himself from the ordinary rhythms of learning to know another person. Intimacy is a quality that can only be explored through time, and the same is true of the qualities of trust and belief in each other that are so much a part of it. Those people who believe that intimacy can be reached in an instant are preaching a superficial version of love that can only disappoint and disillusion those who try it that way. And there are many preachers of instant intimacy, from those who feel that deep love comes out of a few hours in an encounter group to those who think that holding hands at the Liturgy really makes people friends with each other.

Love is far more demanding of the best that is in us than the cheap translations of it that blind people to the need for time in which genuine affection can grow. The latest version of it leaves the development of feelings of affection, in some part at least, to the effects of drugs. A great and glowing case can be made for this pharmaceutical breaking down of the barriers between people. The problem here, as it is in any situation in which time is ransomed by some rationalization, is that the individuals are not really reaching each other as much as some projection of themselves onto each other. They feel warm and tender, and they desperately want some warm and tender response in return. When this is not rooted in what they are really like, they have only cruelly deluded themselves, and a lifetime together for people who do not love each other is the longest kind of time known to man.

There is a grim truth in the old adage about the leisure we have for repenting the things we do in haste. So it sadly is for too many persons who have, for whatever reason, lost sight of the profound meaning of time in all its dimensions in the solemn affairs of the human heart. Premarital sex can be urged, as it is quite regularly, but at what price? A great deal of learning about each other in depth may be thereby cut off so that the individuals will have a painfully difficult time of seeing themselves or their sexuality in the perspective of mature love. Almost anything is justified these days on the grounds that it is all right as long as you do not hurt anybody else in the process. But how much hurt are the purveyors of such a philosophy building into the lives of those who readily accept it? And, in the delicate and sensitive balance of human affairs, who can safely judge when we do or do not hurt others? The story of many second marriages is the story of people who learned the hard way of perils of rushing into a first marriage before the relationship had really developed. In fact, this pattern is so common that many observers refer to the first marriage as a kind of trial or test of the individuals involved through which they may learn enough to find a deeper and better relationship later on. There is little doubt that many second marriages, after a brief first mistake, are far more loving and enduring. There is a high price in heartbreak for learning of this kind, and yet the pressures that push people into these marriages grow greater rather than less.

These pressures have a common denominator of wanting to make a short cut through time. They are made up partly of parental wishes, the individual's own anxiety about getting married, and the epidemic problem of falling in love, not with another person, but just with the idea of falling in love. But time, when it is ignored, catches up with us, and nowhere is this more true than in human love. Recently, psychiatrist Ruth Moulton said this:

In a rapidly moving urban vortex like New York City, it is hard to find time for anything extra, especially if it requires leisure and relaxation like lovemaking. It has been said that open-ended expanses of time, uncounted and freely given, are a necessary milieu for love to occur and grow. Time must be made available to explore intimacy, sexual and otherwise. . . . (*Medical Aspects of Human Sexuality*, Jan. 1970, p. 56)

Probably one of the clearest symptoms of the inroads of time on human intimacy has been the increased self-consciousness of man about his sexuality and his progressive isolation of it from the setting of human relationships. Human sexuality is not focused solely on the act of intercourse itself; there is a context of life and relationship and a more intimate context of play and sharing in which the whole meaning of lovers to each other is expressed. A great deal of this is lost in the current emphasis on technique or in the crippled notion of "having sex" that is so popular now. These attitudes develop when there is really nothing in the human relationship of the lovers that can be expressed in their sexuality. Sex can then be divorced from life together; it is a relief from tension, a pleasurable event where anything that creates pleasure is allowable. All this, of course, reflects the emptiness of the emotional content of the relationship. No wonder the emphasis must be on technique. There really isn't anything else for people who have fallen out of love, or who never had the time to fall in love in the first place.

Sexuality is a victim, then, of our hurried pace, but only insofar as its significance is lessened precisely because the relationships it is meant to express have never had time to grow. Psychologist Max Deutsch notes, about the sex manuals, for example:

> Most of the books deal with sexual technique and don't touch on the problems of intimacy or the importance of sexual activity as emotional communication which bridges isolation, reduces anxieties, and shares pleasures. (*Ibid.*, p. 59)

In our twentieth-century rush we have eclipsed the opportunity for deep human relationships to grow and develop and have harvested the bitter fruit of alienation, multiplied divorces, and sexuality that has been drained of its human significance. There is probably no more melancholy evidence of the latter than the studies that reveal how much people have allowed something like television, for example, to substitute for any relationship with each other. It has, for many couples, become an activity that fills and kills time, keeping them somehow together and yet sadly apart at the same time. Sex has new competition from the late show, and television viewing from bed is probably the most sophisticated avoidance mechanism that people who really don't love each other any more have ever developed. What sex there is for these people must then be necessarily hurried, a sad footnote to a world that has lost any sense of the time that is needed for real loving.

It takes time for all the things that are vital to a growing relationship of love. There is a gradual exploration of each other, a discovery of each other's attitudes and opinions, of each other's strengths and weaknesses; a little insight even into the mystery of each other that will only be understood gradually as the years go by. Lovers need time just to be with each other. Indeed, one of the oldest and best tests of love is whether the individuals concerned can really just be with each other, touching and savoring the meaning of life in its simplest and grandest forms together.

Real love takes time if it is to grow strong enough to be independent of time. For timelessness is love's destiny and only through love can man effectively respond to the tyranny of clocks and calendars. Real love puts lovers outside of the limits of time and death. It enables them to conquer separation and the sacrifices that will be required throughout a lifetime of waiting for one another for one reason or another. This kind of love is stronger than time, and, in its final test, it outlasts it.

Lovers learn many lessons about time in their life together. They realize, sooner or later, that the most important things about their relationship take time. Life in love together is not like a flashily edited movie, full of quick cuts and abrupt scene shifts that eliminate the periods of incubation and quiet flowering that are indispensable to growth. Lovers learn to fear time, knowing that it stalks them, taking away their vigor and their dreams, and that it runs out at last for everyone. But those who love in the Spirit can face and enter into the mysteries and contradictions that time imposes on all humans with a conquering faith and hope. They know that the work of the Spirit cannot be altered or destroyed because it lives beyond the challenges and limits of time. Lovers who can accept a life in time begin to understand the meaning of the eternal life that means that their love never comes to an end at all.

AFTERWORD
NEVER IS A BIG WORD

I became somewhat troubled while writing the previous chapters, uneasy because of the word *never* used in the description of love by St. Paul. *The Jerusalem Bible*, a wonderfully readable translation, had it that way, and yet it just did not seem right. The more I thought about it the less I believed that Paul, scarred by shipwreck, courtroom appearances, and inconstant friends, could have used the adverb *never*. *Never* seemed especially inappropriate to describe love, a qualifier with too little give in it for anybody who has ever known love in everyday life.

Never, like *always*, is a big word, one that may safely be used about angels or statues that are changeless because they are not alive. A big word, however, to use about man, a dangerously inaccurate word for such a restless and shifting creature. *Never*, *always*, and other absolutes are the kinds of words people use in their New Year's resolutions. They have a built-in fragility which causes them to shatter quickly in ice-cold January. "Never say never," Harry Truman once said, "because never is a hell of a long time." Indeed, most of us know how big a word *never* is from some experience of our own fallibility.

People find out, for example, that they frequently end up doing the things they said they would *never* do, whether this concerns where they live, the work they do, or even eating again the thing that makes them sick. And people find that it is very difficult to do the things they say they will *always* do. Man is made in the human condition more for exceptions than for a letter-perfect keeping of inflexible resolutions.

That is why it is misleading to say that love is *never* this, or is *always* that. This is not to excuse the human defects or the faults that make it hard to apply these words to the life of man. It is, however, to recognize that the Spirit of love operates in the human condition where there are gaps in the best of lives and where our scars show that we heal incompletely from the wounds of living. When you say *never* you eliminate any margin for error. The Christian life, however, has wide margins and unlimited forgiveness for those who fall off center now and then. Of its very essence Christian love tolerates mistakes and failures; its most incredible strength is that it bridges gaps and that it pulls the flawed material of life gently together again. Love, if it is anything, is the power the Spirit gives us to respond in the human situation where we are always falling short or not quite measuring up. Love links people in the constantly shifting experience of life in which they can hurt and disappoint each other even after they have said, "I'll *never* hurt you again," or "I'll *always* be kind and gentle."

Lovers make mistakes all the time and constantly sense the tremors of their own shortcomings even as they try their best to overcome them. The ideal of Christian love is not one of rigid perfection, free of all blemishes and unseemly thoughts. The miracle of Christian love is that it is a gift to sinners who can actively accept each other as less than perfect and who thereby redeem each other continually. They keep reaching out, they keep trying to understand, and they keep growing together at the same time.

People who love each other recognize the tension that accompanies their imperfection. They know that they are not immune to anger, or the pull of other attractions, or the feeling of suddenly being distant from one another. what love does is enable them to handle all these common experiences of life and to integrate them without letting them infect and destroy their life together. Love lets people face conflict, even competition at times, without making every situation of stress a battle to the death. Through the power of love people work through the difficulties of life and achieve a new and higher ground of maturity together. The great thing about love is that it is made for and only found among ordinary, mistake-making people.

One of the big problems connected with love in our day is this inability or refusal to work things out when difficulties arise. There are those who do not even realize just how much working out of things goes into any truly loving relationship. At times the need to work through experiences of growth and the very presence of love seem coextensive. This joint effort to understand and to embrace together some new development is a sign that love is alive. If we rephrased one of our earlier questions and asked, "What do lovers do all day?" the answer might well be, "Work through the problems of life."

And the problems of life make quite a long list. They range from the way money is spent to the time supper is served. A fair rule of thumb is that anything people can have a fight about is something they can also work out less violently. George Bach and Peter Wyden have recently suggested (*The Intimate Enemy*, New York, William Morrow & Company, Inc., 1969) that good fights are important for a healthy marriage. They mean, of course, that the non-fighters are just as angry but choose to sulk in separate tents, drifting out of relationship by avoiding combustible subjects. The possible misunderstanding here, as it is with certain forms of group therapy, is to value the fight or the confrontation for its own sake. This is a dangerous missing of the point, dangerous because arguments in themselves are not necessarily as productive of growth as they are expressive of violence.

What is important is the fact that people in love touch and cross each other's lives in a hundred intimate ways every day. Everything makes a difference because everything, especially the little things that get into our love songs, conveys or can seem to convey a deeper attitude of the one for the other. As people live closely they discover more about each other, some of it good and some of it bad. There are countless sources of possible tension as life sweeps along with its melancholy gifts of debts, worry, and wrinkles. Lovers find their growth in the midst of all this, in the reassessment of their ambitions and of each other; in the adjustment to disappointment, illness, or bad luck; in finding that there is really no end to facing together the constantly reappearing problems of life and growth. It is in sharing all of this together that lovers grow strong even though they can still grow weary. Working through difficulties can seem at times to be all there is to life. This growth together makes lovers far more sensitive and tender, and much more alive to each other. The greatest witness to the meaning of loving redemption comes from couples who know the difference between the breadth of unexamined romance and the depth of love that has been tried by life. There is something solid about couples like this, something peaceful and secure, the prize of the Spirit that is given to those who work through life together.

Sin may consist in the refusal to be redemptive in the human condition. Its true face may only be seen when people give up on each other, letting life fall apart because they will not love enough to pull it back together again. The worst sin of all is to disdain the human condition, to turn away from the demands of love, and not to care any more. This is indeed to sin against the Spirit. Sin is a terrible estrangement from the human setting, a rejection of

the simple tasks of reconciliation and forgiveness, a refusal to love enough to make each other whole.

Christianity says that there is hope, even for mankind
that is so weighed down with a consciousness of everything it can do wrong. This hope springs from the saving
power of love that is stronger than the faults of men. One
thinks of Martin Buber's translation of the Hasidic
parable:

> [He] sat among peasants in a village inn and listened
> to their conversation. Then he heard how one asked the
> other, "Do you love me?" And the latter answered, "Now,
> of course, I love you very much." But the first regarded
> him sadly and reproached him for such words: "How can
> you say you love me? Do you know, then, my faults?" And
> then the other fell silent, and silent they sat facing each
> other, for there was nothing more to say. He who truly
> loves knows, from the depths of his identity with the other,
> from the root ground of the other's being he knows where
> his friend is wanting. This alone is love. (*I and Thou*, New
> York, Charles Scribner's Sons, 1958, p. 248)

The Spirit makes it possible for lovers who have
wounded each other to bring again a healing presence to
each other. It means that we can make up for our small-
ness, our jealousies, and all our broken resolutions, not by a
new and unrealistic pledge never to fall again, but by a
willingness to take up the task of loving again. Real love
begins when we are ready to forgive each other and help
each other to do better the next time, not when we expect
each other to go through life with all our lines letter-
perfect. Christian love is not perfect. Nothing meant to
grow is ever perfect at any one moment. The life of the
Spirit is only an approximation of *never* and *always*, and
its glory is revealed in the life to the full that it makes
available for every man.

I was relieved when I asked a scripture scholar friend of
mine about *never* in Paul's description of love. He said

that Paul did not mean never, that he was merely expressing a negative, and while the translation was beautiful, it was a little free. Relieved, yes, and challenged again to turn back to the demands of loving in my own life, more aware than ever of the frailty of our passage together through this world, and more mindful of how much the human family needs our friendship and love.

Nothing will ever match the sudden view we got of ourselves when the pictures of the first earthrise were transmitted from the moon. The other planets hang like stones in the silence of space; we alone, riding the green and blue good earth around the sun, are alive; we alone know the pain and joy of love; we alone can breathe the Spirit of love on each other and give life. We are, for better or worse, with all our shapes and sizes, little prides and big hates, a community together. And the Christian impulse of love bids us now to reach out again to each other, undiscouraged by our past failures, and undismayed by our present imperfections. The Spirit moves us all to take another look at each other and to see deeply the whole meaning and purpose of creation in each other's longings. We are called, even as the Lord said, "to be friends," and it is in the dying that this asks of us that we find and redeem each other.